The
RAJA YOGA
SUTRAS
of Patanjali

D1598952

Translation & Commentary

Swami Jyotirmayananda

YOGA RESEARCH FOUNDATION

CENTER FOR INTEGRAL YOGA

AIMS AND OBJECTIVES

1. To disseminate the essence and mystical meaning of all *Vedantic* Scriptures and the Scriptures of the world, revealing thereby that "Truth is One - Sages and Saints speak of it in different ways."

2. To emphasize the oneness in Creation and cultivate a Spirit that communes with the Ocean of Universal Awareness in the spirit of the *Vedantic* axiom - *"Vasudeva Kutumbakam"* - this world is our family.

3. To introduce to the world the time-proven philosophy of Integral Yoga to bring about the highest culture that humanity can attain.

4. To serve humanity by raising human consciousness through teaching the technique of mastering the mind and following the principles of "simple living and high thinking."

5. To promote the understanding that the ultimate purpose of life is Self-Realization, and to offer powerful and time-tested techniques for attaining it.

6. To demonstrate that one can live in this stressful world, and yet rise above it by learning to use every circumstance in one's life to their advantage.

7. To make available to all, the means to attain a healthy body through *Hatha Yoga* exercises, and *Pranayama* (techniques for breathing correctly).

8. To train the mind to be focused, peaceful, and relaxed, and to go beyond self-limiting concepts in order to discover one's infinite potential.

9. To teach the art of meditation to enable one to render the mind acquiescent, and ultimately to learn how to transcend the body and the mind to experience the super-conscious state of *samadhi.*

10. To publish and make available through books and all media possible, teachings of the highest order, drawn from the ancient wisdom of *Vedanta*, and expressed with rare intuition by the Enlightened Master - Sri Swami Jyotirmayananda.

The Raja Yoga Sutras of Pantanjali
Copyright © 1978 by Swami Jyotirmayananda
All rights reserved.

Yoga Research Foundation
6111 S.W. 74th Avenue
Miami, Florida 33143 U.S.A.
Tel: (305) 666-2006
www.yrf.org

ISBN: 978-0-934664-38-7

Cover Design: Sushila Oliphant

Printed in the United States

PUBLISHER'S NOTE

There is no study so inspiring in the world as the study of the mind, its latent powers, the methods of its control, and its spiritual enlightenment. From remote antiquity to the present day, people have been striving to fathom the depths of the mind, and to channelize mental energy for solving various problems of life.

Centuries before Christ, Sage Patanjali presented the study of mind in the form of aphorisms (Sutras) based upon the experiences and findings of ancient seers. The Sutras literally mean "threads," so called because they thread numerous thoughts together in a succinct manner, allowing an aspirant to easily commit them to memory, and to dwell upon them according to his convenience. And it is because of this Sutra style of writing that even when printing was not possible, people retained the scriptures through memory. This is also the reason why the Sutras retained their original purity; they have been passed on from century to century. undiluted, undistorted and unadulterated. However, due to the brevity of their form, without proper guidance it is difficult to understand the teachings contained in them.

The Raja Yoga Sutras give the profoundest insight into the total workings of the mind. It is amazing how, when this profound text of mystic psychology is studied, facts of the mind are revealed which are yet to be recognized, appreciated and admired by the leading psychologists and parapsychologists of today.

Various commentaries exist on these Sutras, but most of them have ignored the practical need of aspirants. This book, originating from the inspiring pen of Author Sri Swami Jyotir Maya Nanda, was especially written so that anyone can put this unsurpassed teaching into practice in his daily life.

Raja Yoga forms the foundation of all systems of Yoga, in spite of the apparent differences that exist among their philosophies. The importance of the Raja Yogic system of concentration, meditation and Samadhi is unanimously accepted by all systems — advancement in Karma Yoga, Bhakti Yoga, Jnana Yoga, or in a blend of these Yogas, or in Kundalini Yoga, in Tantra Yoga, or in whatever form of Yoga choosen, the eight limbs of Yoga need to be practised as outlined in these Sutras.

Various practical methods have been given in this book to calm the agitated mind, to cultivate virtues, and to root out the bitter complexes of the past that are lodged in the unconscious mind. Anyone who studies this book can become an expert psychoanalyst for himself, and can handle his psychological problems in an effective manner, and in turn, will naturally become an inspiration to others around him. Just as it is impossible for a flower to bloom without spreading its fragrance to its neighborhood, much in the same manner it is impossible for a human being to discover the treasure of spiritual values deep within his soul through mastery over the mind without sharing it with others around him.

In fact, self-culture is the most effective form of serving humanity. Men like Buddha, Jesus, Moses, and Mohammed were great Yogis of the past. Ramana

Maharshi, Ramakrishna Paramahamsa, Mahatma Gandhi, Sri Swami Sivananda and others were great Yogis of recent times. Through their shining examples they have demonstrated the far-reaching results that are possible by attaining mastery over the mind and senses.

As presented by Sri Swami Jyotir Maya Nanda, this is a concise text dealing with Raja Yoga, which includes the workings of the mind, the method of controlling the thoughts, desires and sentiments, the art of cultivating virtuous qualities, the mystic secret of unfolding the great psychic powers, and ultimately, the technique of attaining Self-realization — the state of perfect freedom from the cycles of birth and death.

This book is indeed a priceless treasure for aspirants desirous of attaining spiritual advancement. Even those who do not wish to take up a serious path leading to Self-realization, but who are bent upon attaining a moderate degree of success and prosperity in life, will be immensely benefited by this book.

May you discover the boundless resources of mental energy within yourself, and thus live a life bathed in the light of wisdom and bliss.

Swami Lalitananda

DEDICATION

योगेन चित्तस्य पदेन वाचां मलं शरीरस्य च वैद्यकेन ।
योऽपाकरोत्तं प्रवरं मुनीनां पतञ्जलिं प्राञ्जलिरानतोऽस्मि ॥

This book is humbly dedicated to Sage Patanjali, who, by writing a great work of Sanskrit grammar, brought purification in human speech; by presenting a work on medicine, promoted the purification of the body; and through his marvelous work of Raja Yoga Sutras, showed the art of purifying the mind. My adorations to Sage Patanjali!

CONTENTS

INDEX

PICTURES & ILLUSTRATIONS

INTRODUCTION

Because of the universality of its teachings, *Raja Yoga* literally means Royal Yoga. No matter what religion or faith you may belong to, or what philosophical system you may pursue, you need to control your mind and to develop the power of concentration. Even those who lack religious beliefs recognize the importance of possessing a healthy mind in a healthy body, and *Raja Yoga* has abundant practical lessions in this direction.

No one knows when Sage *Patanjali* existed on Indian soil, but it is evident that these Sutras were written by him centuries before Christ. Tradition has it that these Sutras ultimately proceeded from *Hiranyagargha* (the Cosmic Mind), and were compiled by Sage *Patanjali* for the benefit of mankind.

Raja Yoga is an unparalleled work of ancient psychology and parapsychology. Unlike the clinical methods adopted by psychology today, the Yogis of antiquity discovered the mental laws through their inward experience of concentration, meditation and *Samadhi*. While modern psychology is concerned with normalizing the human personality, *Raja Yoga* psychology beckons the human mind to ascend the glorious heights of Superconsciousness.

The philosophers and mystics of ancient Greece, Persia, Arabia, Egypt and other civilizations were considerably influenced by the teachings of *Raja Yoga*. And it has continued to spread its benevolent influence through the thinkers of recent times, and is being recognized more and more all over the world.

The explanations presented in this book are intended for aspirants who do not want to be lost in the maze of intellectual speculations, but who want to evolve spiritually by adopting a practical course of spiritual disciplines. May you practise Yoga and find for yourself the joys of possessing a mind that is controlled, senses that are mastered, and a spirit that communes with the ocean of universal awareness. May God bless you!

Swami Jyotir Maya Nanda

Author Swami Jyotir Maya Nanda

SAMADHI PAD

Sutra 1

अथ योगानुशासनम्

ATHA YOGA ANUSHASANAM.

ATHA: Now. YOGA: Of Yoga. ANUSHASANAM: Exposition.

Meaning

Now we commence the exposition of Yoga.

Explanation

The term *Atha* is indicative of auspiciousness and the commencement of the text.

Anushasana refers to the following points which are elaborated in the text of *Raja Yoga*: 1. Characteristics of Yoga, 2. Different disciplines of Yoga, 3. Means to the attainment of Yoga, and 4. Fruit of Yoga — Liberation or Self-realization.

Mind is the cause of bondage and release. *Raja Yoga*, therefore, is of universal importance, because it deals with the secrets of the mind and its control. Once one has understood the ways of controlling the mind and drawing energy from the cosmic source, there is nothing impossible for one to acquire.

Since *Raja Yoga* describes the universal vows, such as *Ahimsa* (non-violence), *Satya* (truthfulness), *Brahmacharya* (continence) and so forth, it is not in conflict with any of the religions of the world. Rather, it is the most important science guiding one along the path of life to the goal of Self-realization.

Sutra 2

योगश्चित्तवृत्तिनिरोधः

YOGASH CHITTA VRITTI NIRODHAH.

YOGAH: Yoga. **CHITTA:** Mind-stuff. **VRITTI:** Thought-waves. **NIRODHAH:** Control, Supression or Cessation.

Meaning

Yoga is the cessation of the thought-waves (modifications) of the mind-stuff.

Explanation

This Sutra defines "Yoga." From a general point of view, Yoga comes from the Sanskrit root *Yuj*, which means "to join," and implies the union of the soul with God.

Whatever discipline is adopted to bring about this union is also called Yoga.

There are four main Yogas: 1. Yoga of Wisdom, 2. Yoga of Devotion, 3. Yoga of Action, and 4. Yoga of Meditation. The present book deals with the Yoga of Meditation, which is also known as *Raja Yoga* — the Royal Yoga.

In *Raja Yoga*, the emphasis is given to the control of the modifications of the mind. Therefore, Yoga has been defined as "The cessation of the thought-waves (modifications) of the mind-stuff."

Chitta is the mind-stuff. The concept of *Chitta* in *Raja Yoga* is very profound. The full implications of the *Chitta* will be explained later, but at the outset it is important to understand that the *Chitta* refers to all the functions of the mind: conscious, subconscious and unconscious.

A *Vritti* is a thought-wave and is the function of the *Chitta*. All experiences in human life — sleep, dream, waking, death and rebirth — are brought about by the *Vrittis* of the *Chitta*. These *Vrittis* are broadly divided into five types: perception, misconception, imagination, memory and sleep. *(RAJA YOGA: I, 5-6)*

Nirodha or cessation of the *Vrittis* is a significant term. By the practice of the lower and higher *Samadhis* (states of superconsciousness), a Yogi detaches himself from the *Chitta* and is no longer associated with the mind.

Sutra 3

तदा द्रष्टुः स्वरूपेऽवस्थानम्

TADA DRASHTUH SWARUPE AVASTHANAM.

TADA: Then. DRASHTUH: Of the Seer. SWARUPE: Essential Nature (in the). AVASTHANAM: Establishment or resting.

Meaning

Then the Seer rests in his Essential Nature.

Explanation

Just as a person is able to see his face clearly in a clean mirror, in the same way, a person discovers his real nature through the purified mirror of the *Chitta*. Then he is no longer caught in the illusions of the mind.

As an absolute master of the mind, he operates through the mind until the termination of his fructifying Karma; and, even while operating through the mind, he is no longer attached to the objects of the world. He is a *Sthita Prajna* (one established in wisdom) of the *Gita*. *(II, 55-72)*

Sutra 4

वृत्तिसारूप्यमितरत्र

VRITTI SARUPYAM ITARATRA.

VRITTI: Thought-wave. SARUPYAM: Identification. ITARATRA: At other times.

Meaning

At other times, "the Seer" is identified with the thought-waves.

Explanation

He who has not succeeded in controlling the mental modifications (*Vrittis*) continues to be identified with the moods of the mind determined by the three *Gunas* (modes of nature) that operate through the *Chitta*. When *Sattwa* arises, the mind is calm and peaceful; when *Rajas* arises, it is restless and agitated by many desires; and, when *Tamas* predominates, it is dull and passive. But a Yogi who is established in the Self is no longer identified with these moods. He is the *Gunatita* — one who has transcended the *Gunas*. *(GITA: XIV, 21-27)*

The *Vrittis* or thought-waves that arise during *Sattwa* are called *Shanta* or peaceful. During *Rajas*, they are called *Ghora* or agitated; and during *Tamas*, *Mudha* or dull.

There are five states of the *Chitta* —

1. *Mudha* — dull. When *Tamas* is rising, there is a tendency towards all that is sinful, gross and negative in life. It manifests in sleep, drowsiness, laziness and inertia.

2. *Kshipta* — distracted or fickle state of mind. It is inclined to virtue and vice, good and evil.

3. *Vikshipta* — partially distracted state of mind. A person in this state of mind is increasingly inclined to virtue. However, in the presence of obstacles and temptations, he can slip back to the lower states of the mind.

4. *Ekagrata* — one-pointedness. This is the purified state of mind which belongs to Yogis. The practice of meditation and *Samadhi* is meant to bring about this state. When this state is perfected, one attains intuitional knowledge (*Viveka Khyati*) which reveals the difference between the *Chitta* (mind-stuff) and the *Purusha* (the spirit in its essential glory).

5. *Niruddha* — Controlled state. A Yogi having discovered himself as the Spirit is no longer dependent upon the *Chitta* and its functions. He then

enters into *Asamprajnata Samadhi* or the highest *Samadhi* which gives rise to the state of *Kaivalya* or Liberation.

The first three states, *Mudha, Kshipta* and *Vikshipta*, belong to the worldly-minded people. The last two states, *Ekagrata* and *Niruddha*, belong to the Yogis. During these last two states, a Yogi no longer identifies himself with the *Vrittis* of the mind. These *Vrittis* are further explained in the following Sutra.

Sutra 5

वृत्तयः पञ्चतय्यः क्लिष्टाक्लिष्टाः

VRITTAYAH PANCHATAIYYAH KLISHTA-AKLISHTAH.

VRITTI: Thought-waves. **PANCHATAIYYAH:** Of five types. **KLISHTA:** Painful. **AKLISHTAH:** Not-painful.

Meaning

Vrittis or thought-waves are of five types: (some) painful and (others) not-painful.

Explanation

The innumerable thoughts of the mind can be broadly divided into five types, the names and explanations of which are given in the following Sutras.

These five types of *Vrittis* are either *Klishta* (productive of pain) or *Aklishta* (destructive of pain). *Klishta Vrittis* intensify ignorance, egoism, attachment, hatred, and fear of death, and all that is related to these basic afflictions. *(RAJA YOGA: II, 3)*

Aklishta Vrittis arise on the basis of the practice of the eight limbs of Yoga, which lead to the state of Self-realization or Liberation. *(RAJA YOGA: II, 29)*

Sutra 6

प्रमाणविपर्ययविकल्पनिद्रास्मृतयः

PRAMANA VIPARYAYA VIKALPA NIDRA SMRITAYAH.

PRAMANA: Right knowledge. VIPARYAYA: Wrong knowledge or misconception. VIKALPA: Imagination. NIDRA: Sleep. SMRITI: Memory.

Meaning

These are the five types of *Vrittis* (thought-waves): Right knowledge, Wrong knowledge, Imagination, Sleep and Memory.

Explanation

These *Vrittis* are being explained in the following Sutras. The next Sutra describes the three types of *Pramana* (Right knowledge).

Sutra 7

प्रत्यक्षानुमानागमाः प्रमाणानि

PRATYAKSHA ANUMANA AGAMAH PRAMANANI.

PRATYAKSHA: Direct perception. ANUMANA: Inference. AGAMA: Testimony. PRAMANANI: Are the types of right knowledge.

Meaning

Direct perception, inference, and testimony are the three types of right knowledge.

Explanation

In order to arrive at the right knowledge of anything, one uses either of the three methods, or two of them or all of the three together.

The first method of direct sense-perception is adopted by the vast majority of people. It is direct sense-object contact. For example, one knows a mango fruit by seeing, tasting and touching it. One knows a chair by feeling, sitting and resting on it. One feels the heat of the sun, the coolness of ice and the sweetness of sugar. One experiences headache, pain, worry, anxiety, happiness or grief directly. These are all examples of *Pratyaksha Pramana* or direct perception.

The second method of arriving at right knowledge is the adoption of inference. We see smoke on a hill, and infer that there must be fire. We see peace and bliss in the face of a Sage and infer there must be the fire of wisdom blazing in his heart. We see power, majesty and glory in the acts of a Sage, and infer that the life of the Spirit must be full of bliss and joy.

The third method is testimony or authority of competent persons. When a scientist says that water is constituted of hydrogen and oxygen, that two atoms of hydrogen and one atom of oxygen go to form one molecule of water, we believe in this on the basis of authority.

When a Sage declares that the life in *Atman* (the Universal Self) is the ocean of joy, that essentially all are divine, that the goal of life is God-realization, and that nothing is impossible for man to acquire through right effort, we believe him on the authority of the intuition of the Sages.

There is yet another example: When a friend who has been to London describes the city and the people, we believe him on the basis of testimony.

Any perception, inference or testimonial knowledge that aids *Vairagya* (dispassion) and directs the mind to the Self within is *Aklishta* or not-painful, but that which intensifies attachment to the objects of the world is called *Klishta* or painful.

Sutra 8

विपर्ययो मिथ्याज्ञानमतद्रूपप्रतिष्ठम्

VIPARYAYO MITHYAJNANAM ATADRUPA PRATISHTHITAM.

VIPARYAYO: Wrong knowledge.
MITHYAJNANAM: Unreal or false knowledge.
ATAD: Not its own. RUPA: Form.
PRATISHTHITAM: Is established.

Meaning

Viparyaya is false knowledge which is not established in the right form of the object.

Explanation

In the case of right knowledge, the *Vritti* or the thought-wave of the *Chitta* is different from the form of the object. The *Chitta* is modified into something different from the object. For instance, in the example of the perception of snake-in-rope, the *Vritti* of the *Chitta* is modified into snake, while the object is different from the snake; it is a mere rope.

Viparyaya or wrong knowledge does not necessarily imply knowledge that is lacking in ethical value. The term "wrong" is used only to differentiate it from *Pramana* or right knowledge.

Even a right knowledge can be painful (*Klishta*). There are various objects in the world that awaken desire in the undisciplined mind. Even though those objects are perceived with the accuracy of perception, yet the very *Pramana Vritti* becomes a channel of increasing impressions of attachment and hatred in the mind.

In the same way, a wrong knowledge can become not-painful (*Aklishta*) as well. The sky is perceived as blue. The blueness in the sky is a wrong perception, but yet it is comfortable to the senses and pleasing to the mind. When the mind meditates upon the blue expansion of the sky, it enjoys serenity and peace. In short, the world around every person is a blend of right and wrong perceptions; and each of these can be good or evil — not-painful or painful.

Sutra 9

शब्दज्ञानानुपाती वस्तुशून्यो विकल्पः

SHABDA JNANANUPATI VASTU SHUNYO VIKALPAH.

SHABDA: Word. JNANANUPATI: Knowledge born of. VASTU SHUNYO: Devoid of object. VIKALPAH: Imagination.

Meaning

That which follows mere words, devoid of reality, is called *Vikalpa* or Imagination.

Explanation

When a person says "wooden doll," "golden ornament," or "*Purusha's* consciousness," he creates an idea that doll is different from wood, or ornament is different from gold, or consciousness is different from *Purusha* (soul). Such imaginary ideas develop on the basis of mere words only. These are the examples of *Vikalpa*.

The difference between *Viparyaya* (wrong knowledge) and *Vikalpa* (imagination) is that in the case of *Viparyaya* there is a misconception pertaining to some existing object. But in the case of *Vikalpa*, the basis is words only, without any existing reality.

Right knowledge is to see a rope in a rope (*Tadrupa Pratishtha*). Wrong knowledge is to see a snake in a rope (*Atadrupa Pratishtha*). Imagination is different from both; it is to imagine with no tangible basis.

Sutra 10

अभावप्रत्ययालम्बना वृत्तिर्निद्रा

ABHAVA PRATYAYA ALAMBANA VRITTIR NIDRA.

ABHAVA: Absence. PRATYAYA: Knowledge of. ALAMBANA: Support. VRITTI: Thought-waves. NIDRA: Sleep.

Meaning

Sleep is that function of the mind which sustains the absence of all knowledge.

Explanation

During sleep, there is no experience of right knowledge, wrong knowledge, imagination, or memory, which go to constitute the realities of daily life. However, when a person wakes up and says, "I enjoyed sleep profoundly," it is because of the *Nidra Vritti* (thought-wave of sleep) that he is able to remember the absence of all practical realities of life and the experience of joy during sleep.

Also, a subtle form of psychological sleep continues to operate in one's daily life. Although one is involved in his day to day realities, he is asleep to many things, which does not allow him to develop a profounder dimension of awareness.

Sleep is painful when it continues to create dullness and inertia, but not-painful when it refreshes a person with a new vitality. Sleep in moderation is enjoined for a Yogi. *(GITA: VI, 17)*

Sutra 11

अनुभूतविषयासंप्रमोषः स्मृतिः

ANUBHUTA VISHAYA ASAMPRAMOSHAH SMRITIH.

ANUBHUTA: Perceived. VISHAYA: Object. ASAMPRAMOSHAH: Not hiding. SMRITIH: Memory.

Meaning

Memory is the recollection of an object already experienced, without any distortion.

Explanation

Dream is a conditioned projection of the waking state. Therefore, to the dreaming subject, his dream consists of the same five types of *Vrittis*. Some commentators classify dream as *Smriti* or memory. However, memory expressing as dream is totally different from the memory in the waking state.

That type of the Memory-*Vritti* which induces dispassion (*Vairagya*) and devotion is *Aklishta* or not-painful. The memory of objects which causes passion, attachment and craving is *Klishta* or painful.

These five types of *Vrittis* comprise all experiences of a person during the state of bondage. He needs to control *Klishta Vrittis* (negative thoughts) by *Aklishta Vrittis* (positive thoughts). And finally, having developed intuitive vision, he must rise beyond the very basis of all thoughts — the mind-stuff.

The manner of controlling the *Vrittis* is described in the following Sutra.

Sutra 12

अभ्यासवैराग्याभ्यां तन्निरोधः

ABHYASA VAIRAGYABHYAM TANNIRODHAH.

ABHYASA VAIRAGYABHYAM: By repeated practice and dispassion. **TAD:** Their. **NIRODHAH:** Control.

Meaning

These *Vrittis* are controlled by practice and dispassion.

Explanation

In order to control the *Vrittis* (thoughts) of the mind, there are two effective methods, *Abhyasa* (repeated practice) and *Vairagya* (dispassion).

The *Chitta* (mind-stuff) is compared to a river which flows both ways: towards *Samsara* (world-process) by the path of attachment, infatuation, ignorance and non-discrimination, and towards *Kaivalya* or Liberation through the path of discriminative knowledge and detachment.

The natural, outgoing tendencies of the *Chitta* are curbed by *Vairagya*. The internal Godward flow of the mind is strengthened by *Abhyasa*.

Just as a bird flies in the sky with the help of two wings, even so the soul flies in the sky of freedom or Liberation with the help of *Vairagya* and *Abhyasa*.

Lord *Krishna* says to *Arjuna* in the *Bhagavad Gita*, "Indeed this restless mind is difficult to control; but it can be brought under one's control by the exercise of *Abhyasa* and *Vairagya*." *(VI, 35)*

The nature of *Abhyasa* and the means to its perfection are described in the following two Sutras.

TWOFOLD STREAM OF THE MIND

* Mind flows in two directions: To the desert of the world-process and to the ocean of Liberation; the former is checked by Vairagya (dispassion) and the latter is promoted by Abhyasa (repeated practice).

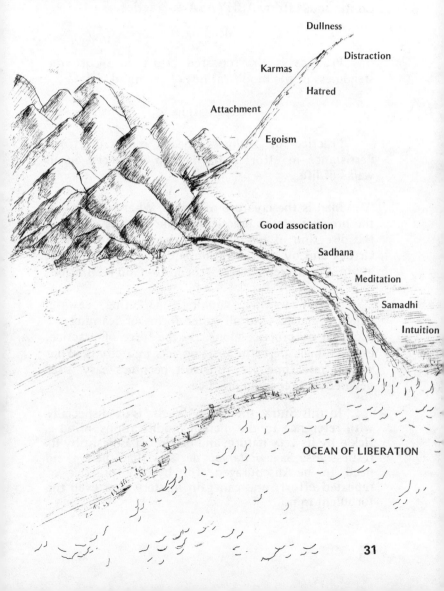

DESERT OF THE WORLD-PROCESS

Dullness

Distraction

Karmas

Hatred

Attachment

Egoism

Good association

Sadhana

Meditation

Samadhi

Intuition

OCEAN OF LIBERATION

Sutra 13

तत्र स्थितौ यत्नोऽभ्यासः

TATRA STHITAU YATNO ABHYASAH.

TATRA: Of these. STHITAU: Steadiness. YATNO: Continuous effort. ABHYASAH: Practice.

Meaning

Practice is the repeated effort to secure the steadiness of the modifications of the mind.

Explanation

Practice of *Abhyasa* means repeated effort. Persistance in effort is the key to all success in all walks of life.

Man is the creature of habits. What he is now is the product of the practices of the past. By changing the direction of his effort, by the practice of divine virtues and by concentration and meditation, he can attain the supreme success in life — God-realization.

Study, writing, cooking, marketing, sewing, dancing, music, and all other forms of learning are acquired by practice alone. By the force of practice, even animals perform amazing acts in a circus. What was at one time very difficult becomes easy after devoted and repeated practice.

In this Sutra, the term *Abhyasa* is used specially with reference to the mental modifications. Mind is fickle by its very nature, and baffles an aspirant by its restlessness. Sage *Patanjali* declares that there is no need to be discouraged, for by the practice of repeated effort, one can gain mastery over even the turbulent mind.

The next Sutra gives the method of rendering *Abhyasa* steady.

Sutra 14

स तु दीर्घकालनैरन्तर्यसत्कारासेवितो दृढभूमिः

SA TU DEERGHAKALA NAIRANTARYA SATKARA SEVITO DEERGHA BHUMIH.

SA TU: This practice. DEERGHAKALA: For a long time. NAIGANTARYA: Without break, or ceaselessly. SATKARA: With faith and devotion. SEVITA: When practised well. DEERGHA BHUMIH: Firm ground or stable.

Meaning

The aforementioned *Abhyasa* (repeated practice) when practised well without break, for a long time, and with perfect faith and devotion, becomes firmly established.

Explanation

The following are the three conditions for perfecting *Abhyasa* —

1. For a long time: One should not set a time limit for his spiritual practice. Just as a person continues to eat day by day, in the same way, he must continue to practise Yoga day by day. Aspirants are in different levels of evolution: some attain success in a short time; others take a longer time. One should develop tenacity in his nature, and day by day continue to intensify positive impressions.

When a person sows a mango seed in the ground, he needs to allow time for it to sprout and to grow into a tree, for it to blossom and to yield fruit. In the same way, an aspirant must await the fullness of time for the fruit of Self-realization.

2. Without any break: The second important condition is that one must carry on one's effort without any break. Off and on practice does not bear fruit quickly. The *Samskaras* (impressions) of sense-enjoyments exist in the *Chitta* (mind-stuff) of man, and it is difficult to destroy them in a short time. Practice must be prolonged and protracted.

To practise for a month and then to leave it for ten days, then to practise for three months and then to leave it for a month, is practice done with breaks. One cannot attain steadiness of mind even after practising in this way for a long period of time. Off and on practice is of little value.

3. With faith and devotion: Even if a person practises ceaselessly for a long time without any break, he will not be able to attain success if he is devoid of faith and devotion. These two qualifications are of utmost importance for an aspirant. Faith leads to intense aspiration, aspiration draws divine grace, and grace removes impediments from the path and bestows immortality.

The next Sutra now describes the second method of controlling the mind — *Vairagya*.

Sutra 15

दृष्टानुश्रविकविषयवितृष्णस्य वशीकारसंज्ञा वैराग्यम्

DRISHTA ANUSHRAVIK VISHAYA VAITRISHNASYA VASHIKARA SAJNA VAIRAGYAM.

DRISHTA: Seen. ANUSHRAVIK: Heard. VISHAYA: Objects of enjoyment. VAITRISHNASYA: Of him who is free from hankering or craving. VASHIKARA: Control. SAJNA: Name. VAIRAGYAM: Dispassion.

Meaning

Those who do not have hankering for objects seen or heard of, have attained lower *Vairagya* named *Vashikara* or control.

Explanation

The objects of enjoyment are of two types —

1. *Drishta* — objects seen in this world and objects of sense-perception in daily life, for example, music, touch, smell, forms, taste, wealth, family, fame, etc..

2. *Anushravic* — objects heard of from the *Vedas* or other scriptures. These are again of two types —

(a) Objects attainable after death, as, for example, the objects of heaven or experiences of the higher worlds. These objects are infinitely more refined than the objects of this world, but they are temptations for those who desire Liberation.

(b) Objects attainable in life through change in the mode of one's consciousness. For example, Yogis, by the power of their concentrated minds, are able to enjoy divine smell, divine taste, divine music, and other divine perceptions.

By the force of discrimination, however, an aspirant should understand the defects of all objective pleasures of the world, whether physical or astral, seen or unseen, and he should keep his mind ever fixed on God.

Vairagya (dispassion) cannot be developed overnight; it grows by degrees. There are four stages in the development of *Vairagya* —

1. *Yatamanam* — Striving Stage: The impurities in the form of impressions of love and hatred drive the senses to sense-objects. These sense-objects in turn intensify the impressions of love and hatred (*Raga* and *Dwesha*).

In this first stage of *Vairagya*, the aspirant thinks again and again of the defects of attachment and hatred, like and dislike. He repeatedly thinks of the ensnaring nature of objects. He endeavors to renounce attachment and hatred by keeping away from the objects, by practice of virtues, by good association, repetition of the Lord's Name, and many similar methods.

2. *Vyatirekam* — Differentiating Stage: Through the practice of *Yatamanam*, the aspirant begins to become conscious of different degrees of dispassion developed towards different objects. He may have great control over his tongue, but may not have the

same degree of control over his sight. He may have a great craving for reading novels, but may have little craving for attending the theater.

He is aware of degrees of dispassion. He understands that many impure *Samskaras* (impressions) of the mind have been removed, and many remain to be removed.

3. *Ekendriyam* — One-sense Stage: In this stage, the senses are mastered. But the lord of the senses, the mind, is still uncontrolled. The impurities of the mind — the impressions of *Raga* and *Dwesha* — have become so weak that they cannot move the senses to the sense-objects.

But the *Vasanas* or the subtle desires still remain. Mind is the only sense* that troubles the aspirant at this stage.

4. *Vashikaram* — Controlled Stage: When the subtle impurities of the mind are removed and the mind has regained serenity and perfect balance, it is known as *Vashikara* (controlled). Mind is not distracted in the presence of celestial or noncelestial objects.

There is perfect indifference towards all enjoyments, because there is no subtle desire left in the mind. The senses become meek. But yet, the impressions of the afflictions are not burnt up. They are destroyed only by *Asamprajnata Samadhi* (the highest superconsciousness) brought about by *Para Vairagya* or supreme dispassion.

---

* According to Raja Yoga, mind or Manas is placed in the category of the Indriyas, which are 11 — 5 subtle senses of perception, 5 subtle organs of action, and Manas.

This lower *Vairagya* helps in the attainment of *Para Vairagya*. This *Vairagya* is an aid in the practice of concentration, meditation, and lower *Samadhi*.

The foregoing Sutra described *Apara Vairagya* (lower dispassion), and now the next Sutra takes up the description of *Para Vairagya* or supreme dispassion.

Sutra 16

तत्परं पुरुषख्यातेर्गुणवैतृष्ण्यम्

TAT PARAM PURUSHAKHYATER GUNA VAITRISHNYAM.

TAT: That. PARAM: Supreme. PURUSHAKHYATER: Knowledge of the Spirit. GUNA: The modes of nature. VAITRISHNYAM: Non-attachment.

Meaning

Supreme dispassion is that state in which even the attachment to the modes of *Prakriti* (Nature) drops owing to the knowledge of the *Purusha* (Spirit).

Explanation

In *Apara Vairagya* (lower dispassion), one develops detachment towards all objects seen and unseen. The mind is focused on one point, and its tendency to outer objects is mastered. The *Chitta* or the mind-stuff has attained the modification of one-pointedness. In other words, it flows to one object alone.

When lower *Samadhi* is perfected (in *Sasmita Samadhi*), one attains *Purusha Jnana*, the Knowledge of the Self. By the force of this knowledge, a Yogi develops distaste towards even the three *Gunas* (*Sattwa*, purity; *Rajas*, activity; and *Tamas*, inertia) and their effects. This is known as *Para Vairagya* or supreme dispassion, which is the direct means to attain *Asamprajnata Samadhi* (the highest *Samadhi*).

Vairagya is the seed. *Samprajnata Samadhi* (lower superconsciousness) is the sprout. *Viveka Khyati* (spiritual knowledge) is the tree. *Dharma Megha* (cloud of virtue) brings the rain. *Para Vairagya* (supreme dispassion) is the flower. *Asamprajnata Samadhi* (supreme superconsciousness) is the fruit. *Kaivalya* (Liberation) is the ripe fruit.

The explanations of these are given in the following Sutras.

Sutra 17

वितर्कविचारानन्दास्मितानुगमात्संप्रज्ञातः

VITARKA VICHARA ANANDA ASMITA ANUGAMAT SAMPRAJNATAH.

VITARKA: Argumentative. VICHARA: Reflective or deliberative. ANANDA: Joyous. ASMITA: "Am"-ness, pertaining to the source of ego. ANUGAMAT: Followed by. SAMPRAJNATAH: Lower *Samadhi* or superconsciousness in which the intellect, due to its transparency, reveals the truth of the object of meditation in its different planes.

Meaning

Samprajnata Samadhi (lower form of superconsciousness) is that which is followed by argument, deliberation or reflection, joy, and "Am"-ness.

Explanation

The ladder of Yoga contains various rungs, and the *Samadhis* are the higher rungs. They are the stages of superconsciousness that lead to the attainment of the highest goal of life, *Kaivalya* (Liberation).

Samadhi or the experience of superconsciousness washes away all the impurities from the mirror of mind and grants intuitive vision. *Samadhi* is that philosopher's stone which transforms the reasoning faculty into that of intuition, and intuition, in turn, is the mystic water of life that grants immortality.

Samadhi is that mystic summit from where all is "here" and "now," and the past and future fuse into the roaring waters of the Present. It is that wish-yielding tree that confers all desires. *Samadhi*, verily, is the key to all higher attainments and divine manifestations.

Samadhi comes after *Dhyana* (meditation) and *Dharana* (concentration). *Dharana* is the fixing of the mind on one point, object, idea or center within. It is likened to the focusing of the rays of the sun through a lens.

Samadhi is superconscious absorption in the object of meditation. It is likened to the ignition produced by the lens when focused for a period of time on an object.

That particular experience in which the object of meditation is revealed in various levels in the clear light of *Sattwa* (purity), free from both wrong knowledge and imagination, is *Samprajnata Samadhi*. It is the lower form of superconsciousness which ranges from the gross plane of physical objects to the plane of *Asmita* — the source of ego principle.

When the mind becomes increasingly purer by the practice of *Samadhi*, the Yogi ascends the higher steps of *Samadhi* one after another. A Yogi may choose any object for his initial pracitce of meditation, but as he advances, he is led through the same stages of *Samadhi* until he attains the highest.

A salt doll, wherever dropped in the ocean, becomes one with the ocean. Even so, mind, wherever fixed or concentrated, ultimately leads one to the ascending steps of *Samadhi*.

The lower *Samadhis* correspond to these four planes —

1. *Vitarka Samadhi*. It is *Samadhi* pertaining to the first plane. Here the object of meditation is perceptible by the senses in the gross plane. This *Samadhi* gives rise to an intuitive experience which is totally unique — an experience which has not been seen, heard or inferred before. *Vitarka Samadhi* is of two types:

(a) *Savitarka*. Here *Shabda* (word), *Artha* (form) and *Jnana* (idea) of the object of meditation are confused.

In gross perceptions, the qualities of *Rajas* (activity) and *Tamas* (inertia) bring about misconception and perversion. That is why one is not able to distinguish between the *word*, the *form* of the object referred to by the word, and the *idea* of the object. For instance, when a man says "cow," he does not seriously think that this word is merely a combination of the letters 'c', 'o', and 'w'. When spoken, the *word* resides on the tongue. The *form* of the object "cow" signified by the *word* is different from the *word*; it resides in the barn. And, the *idea* of "cow" being an animal of particular characteristics resides in the mind.

In gross perception, there is a mixture of *word*, *form* and *idea*. As long as this confusion continues and mind has to adopt the method of argumentation and analysis, *Samadhi* arising at this level is called *Savitarka*. A sort of mental argumentation is involved in arriving at the right perception of the object, and therefore, it is called "with argument."

(b) *Nirvitarka*. When the mind fixes itself on the gross object without being confused by *Shabda*, *Artha* and *Jnana*, it is known as *Nirvitarka* or without argumentation.

2. *Vichara Samadhi*. As the gross state of the object is experienced in *Samadhi*, the light of intellect grows brighter. From the very same gross object, there emerges the penetrative vision of the *Tanmatras* (the subtle elements) which go to constitute the

object. The gross object disappears, and in its place these subtle root-elements appear.

When the *Indriyas* (the subtle senses, the subtle organs of action, and mind) and *Tanmatras* are experienced without any misconception or imagination, it is called *Vichara Samadhi*. This *Samadhi* is also of two types: (a) *Savichara* — when there is an awareness of time and space, and (b) *Nirvichara* — when the Yogi remains in the subtle plane, having lost the awareness of time and space.

3. *Sananda Samadhi*. As the persistant practice of *Vichara* renders the mind subtle and extremely purified, the *Ahamkara* (ego-principle) reveals itself. This *Ahamkara* is the source of the *Indriyas* and *Tanmatras*. It is known as *Ananda* (bliss), because it is full of joy.

Sattwa or purity predominates in this experience. One experiences "I am blissful. I am blissful." Yogis who leave their body in this stage attain the state of *Videha* or bodiless state. They experience unalloyed felicity in the astral world for a long, long time.

4. *Sasmita Samadhi*. The experience, "I am blissful" becomes more and more purified as *Sattwa* increases. What then remains is the experience of *"Asmi"* — "I AM."

Asmita is the cause of the ego-principle or *Ahamkara Tattwa*. Those dying in this stage attain a state called *Prakriti Laya* (absorption in *Prakriti* — or absorption in Nature), and enjoy felicity for a long, long time in the heavenly world.

TABLE OF SAMADHIS

COSMIC PLANES	SAMADHIS
Prakriti	Asamprajnata Samadhi
Mahat	Sasmita Samadhi
Ahamkara	Sananda Samadhi
Subtle Elements	Nirvichara Samadhi & Savichara Samadhi
Gross Elements	Nirvitarka Samadhi & Savitarka Samadhi

SUBJECTIVE COUNTERPARTS OF COSMIC PLANES	SAMADHIS
Chitta	Asamprajnata Samadhi
Buddhi	Sasmita Samadhi
Ego	Sananda Samadhi
Mind & Senses	Nirvichara Samadhi & Savichara Samadhi
Body	Nirvitarka Samadhi & Savitarka Samadhi

Sutra 18

विरामप्रत्ययाभ्यासपूर्वः संस्कारशेषोऽन्यः

VIRAM PRATYAYA ABHYASA PURVAH SAMSKARA SHESHONYAH.

VIRAM: The cessation of all *Vrittis* or thought-waves. **PRATYAYA:** The cause (of such cessation, i.e., *Para Vairagya*). **ABHYASA:** Repeated practice. **PURVAH:** Preceding condition. **SAMSKARA SHESHAH:** Residual impression due to the practice of *Para Vairagya*. **ANYAH:** The other (*Asamprajnata Samadhi*).

Meaning

That Yoga (*Asamprajnata Samadhi*) is another: of which the practice of *Viram Pratyaya* (cessation of thought-waves due to *Para Vairagya*) is the preceding state, and *Samskara Shesha* (residual impressions of control) is the suceeding state.

Explanation

The highest rung of *Samprajnata Samadhi* is *Sasmita Samadhi*. This arises when the *Chitta* (mind-stuff) of the Yogi turns away from the ego-center and seeks the source of the ego. Due to increasing purity, a Yogi develops that intuitive vision which reveals the difference between the mind-stuff and the Self. This is known as *Viveka Khyati* (intuitive vision).

As a result of this intuitive vision, a Yogi begins to realize that even the *Chitta* is no longer needed. A mirror serves the purpose of reflecting one's face; after that, it is useless. In the same way, once the

Chitta has reflected the nature of the Self, it must be withdrawn into its universal plane, known as *Prakriti* or Nature.

When a Yogi then detaches himself from the *Chitta*, it is known as *Para Vairagya* (supreme dispassion). The impressions of supreme dispassion are called *Viram Pratyaya* — that which puts an end to all the outgoing modifications of the mind.

Para Vairagya is the direct path to *Asamprajnata Samadhi*, the highest *Samadhi*, in which a Yogi turns away from even the one-pointed *Vritti* of *Viveka Khyati*. A Yogi begins to experience *Niruddha* — the controlled state of the mind-stuff. This gives rise to *Nirodha Samskaras* (impressions of control).

Once a fire has consumed its fuel, it is automatically extinguished. In the same way, once the *Nirodha Samskaras* have destroyed the outgoing impressions, they themselves are automatically effaced. This results in *Kaivalya* or Liberation.

But what happens to the Yogi who, due to some obstacle, stays in the *Sananda* or *Sasmita* state of lower *Samadhi*? What is the future for one who dies before attaining *Kaivalya*? This is explained in the following Sutra.

Sutra 19

भवप्रत्ययो विदेहप्रकृतिलयानाम्

BHAVA-PRATYAYO VIDEHAPRAKRITI-LAYANAM.

BHAVA-PRATYAYO: By the mere cause of human birth (there arises *Samadhi*). VIDEHA-PRAKRITILAYANAM: For those who are merged in *Sananda Samadhi*, as well as those who are merged in *Sasmita Samadhi*.

Meaning

For *Videhas* and *Prakritilayas*, a human birth alone is enough to cause the highest *Samadhi* to arise.

Explanation

Yogis who die having attained the level of *Sananda Samadhi* are called *Videha* (bodiless). They have destroyed their identification with the body, but have not attained the fullness of Self-realization. After death, they enjoy boundless bliss in the plane of the pure mind, and are reborn in a family of Yogis, where they do not need to put forth any effort to enter into *Samadhi*. The very fact of embodiment has exhausted their obstructive Karma, and they enter into *Asamprajnata* without any effort.

The same applies to *Prakritilayas* — Yogis who have attained *Sasmita Samadhi*, but did not go further. After death, they merge themselves into *Prakriti* (Nature) and enjoy the bliss of liberated souls for a long time. But they also must be reborn in order to attain the fullness of Liberation.

For example, the *Aittareya Upanishad* describes how Sage *Vamadeva*, while still in the womb of his mother, declared, "Ah, though still in the womb, I have realized the birth of gods. Many fetters of

Karma had held me in bondage; but I have broken them all. And like a hawk, I have become free to fly in the realms of freedom."

This is an illustration of *Bhava Pratyaya* Yogis, who attain *Samadhi* as spontaneously as young birds learn to fly. But other Yogis, who fell from Yoga without attaining the higher states of *Samadhi*, must take recourse to *Upayas* (spiritual means). This is explained in the following Sutra.

Sutra 20

श्रद्धावीर्यस्मृतिसमाधिप्रज्ञापूर्वक इतरेषाम्

SHRADDHA VIRYA SMRITI SAMADHI PRAJNA PURVAK ITARESHAM.

SHRADDHA: Faith. **VIRYA:** Energy. **SMRITI:** Memory. **SAMADHI:** Superconsciousness. **PRAJNA:** Intuitive vision. **PURVAK:** Along with. **ITARESHAM:** For others.

Meaning

For other Yogis, the highest *Samadhi* is attained gradually by the practice of faith, energy, memory, *Samadhi*, and intuitive vision.

Explanation

Referring to the Yogis who are in lower levels of spiritual evolution, Lord *Krishna* says in the *Gita*: "There he comes in touch with the knowledge acquired in his former body, and strives more than ever for perfection, Oh Son of Kunti." *(VI, 43)*

Unflinching faith in Yoga produced by the purification of the heart is called *Shraddha*. Untiring perseverance and tenacity in the practice of Yoga is known as *Virya*. *Shraddha* leads to *Virya*.

When the Yogi gathers mental strength, he is able to restrain the outgoing impressions of the mind. This causes the revival of good past impressions. This is called *Smriti* (memory). Memory of past Yogic practices aids a Yogi to move forward with greater intensity and momentum.

As a Yogi begins to experience *Samadhi*, he gradually develops the intuitive vision which bestows *Para Vairagya* (supreme dispassion). This leads him on to Liberation.

That some Yogic practitioners succeed in a short time, while others linger for a long time, is explained in the next Sutra.

Sutra 21

तीव्रसंवेगानामासन्नः

TEEBRA SAMVEGANAM ASANNAH.

TEEBRA: Intense. SAMVEGANAM: Momentum of *Vairagya*. ASANNAH: Quick.

Meaning

Those who move with the momentum of intense *Vairagya* attain the highest *Samadhi* quickly.

Explanation

It is increasing dispassion along with the intensity of faith, energy, memory, *Samadhi*, and intuitive vision that leads one to the highest *Samadhi* quickly. The following Sutra elaborates upon this further.

Sutra 22

मृदुमध्याधिमात्रत्वात्ततोऽपि विशेषः

MRIDU-MADHYA-ADHIMATRATWAT TATOPI VISHESHAH.

MRIDU-MADHYA-ADHIMATRATWAT: Because of the degree of *Sadhana* (spiritual practice) being either mild, moderate or intense. (MRIDU — mild, MADHYA — moderate, ADHIMATRA — intense). **TATOPI:** Than that also. **VISHESHAH:** Differentiation.

Meaning

Because of the degree of *Sadhana* being either mild, moderate or intense, Yogis are differentiated (into various categories).

Explanation

Spiritual movement depends upon *Upaya* (faith, energy, memory, *Samadhi* and intuitive vision) and *Samvega* (dispassion or *Vairagya*). A Yogi may be mild, moderate or intense in *Upaya* as well as in *Vairagya*.

If he is mild in *Upaya* and mild in *Vairagya*, his spiritual success will be extremely slow. On the other hand, if he has intense *Upaya* and intense *Vairagya*, he will attain the highest state of Yoga in a short time.

There is yet another secret in attaining *Samadhi* quickly, and is given in the following Sutra.

Sutra 23

ईश्वरप्रणिधानाद्वा

ISHWAR PRANIDHANADVA.

ISHWAR: God. PRANIDHANAT: By surrendering. VA: In addition to this.

Meaning

In addition to this, by surrendering to God (one attracts the highest *Samadhi*).

Explanation

When the human personality is integrated by Yoga, there unfolds the rare blossom of surrender to God.

When a Yogi begins to delight in the love of God, he ascends the higher stages of *Samadhi* without much effort. Spiritual love beckons his soul to the state of Liberation, and he is aided by divine grace.

Lord *Krishna* says in the *Gita*: "Among all Yogis, I consider him to be best of Yogis who worships Me with intense faith, and whose mind is immersed in Me." *(VI, 47)*

51

The nature of God and the method of surrendering to Him is described in the following Sutras.

Sutra 24

क्लेशकर्मविपाकाशयैरपरामृष्टः पुरुषविशेष ईश्वरः

KLESHA KARMA VIPAKA ASHAYAIRA APARAMRISHTAH PURUSHA VISHESHA ISHWARAH.

KLESHA: Afflictions. KARMA: Action. VIPAKA: Fructification of action. ASHAYAIRA: Impressions of action. APARAMRISHTAH: Untouched. PURUSHA VISHESHA: Best of all souls. ISHWARAH: God.

Meaning

God is the best of all souls, and is untouched by the afflictions, Karmas, fructifications of Karmas, and impressions of Karmas.

Explanation

God is the best of all souls, because, while the individual souls are trapped in the bondage of the world-process, God is ever free.

According to Vedanta philosophy, God (*Ishwara*) is a reflection of *Brahman* (the Absolute) in *Maya* (Nature predominated by *Sattwa* or the principle of purity). He controls *Maya* and is not affected by it. *Jiva* (the individual soul), on the other hand, is a reflection of the same Absolute in *Avidya* (Nature predominated by *Rajas* or the principle of activity).

When the *Jiva* overcomes ignorance by knowledge, it communes with *Ishwara* (God), and having gone beyond the veil of *Maya*, discovers its identity with the Absolute.

Instead of going into the various philosophical views about the relationship between God and *Jiva*, *Patanjali Maharshi* adopts the simple understanding that the qualities of the object meditated upon (*Upasya*) reflect in the meditator (*Upasaka*).

If God is meditated upon as the Self beyond all limitations, the soul discovers its spiritual nature detached from all Karmic limitations, and thereby attains release from *Prakriti* (Nature). Keeping Liberation in view as the goal of all Yogic movement, *Patanjali Maharshi* has stated in this Sutra that God is free of *Kleshas*, *Karmas*, *Vipaka* and *Ashaya*. These are explained as follows —

Kleshas (Afflictions): The five *Kleshas* are *Avidya* (ignorance), *Asmita* (egoism), *Raga* (attachment), *Dwesha* (hatred), and *Abhinivesha* (clinging to life). *(RAJA YOGA: II, 3)*

Karmas (Actions): There are three types of actions, good, evil and mixed. *(RAJA YOGA: IV, 7)*

Vipaka (Fructification of Karmas): Actions performed with desire give rise to three types of fruit, *Jati* (birth in a particular class), *Ayu* (life), and *Bhoga* (enjoyments). *(RAJA YOGA: II, 13)*

Ashaya (Impressions of Karmas): Impressions of Karmas that exist in the *Chitta* in seed-form constitute *Ashaya*. These seeds sprout and grow into Karmic fructifications.

An individual soul is affected by the above limitations; but God is free from them. By meditating upon God and surrendering to Him, a Yogi liberates his soul from the fetters of *Prakriti*.

Sutra 25

तत्र निरतिशयं सर्वज्ञबीजम्

TATRA NIRATISHAYAM SARVAJNA-BIJAM.

TATRA: In God. NIRATISHAYAM: Unexcellable (of the highest degree). SARVAJNA-BIJAM: The seed of omniscience.

Meaning

In God, the seed of omniscience unfolds to its highest degree.

Explanation

When a Yogi begins to practise concentration, meditation and *Samadhi*, he discovers the seed of omniscience which gradually begins to unfold in him. As he advances on the path of *Samadhi*, *Sattwa* (purity or luminosity) continues to increase in his mind. Thus, his growing knowledge begins to penetrate the mysteries of all knowable objects.

In such a Yogi, however, this capacity to know intuitively increases and decreases according to the degrees of *Sattwa*. But God is limitless in His omniscience. God is the ocean of knowledge. He is *Chit Swarupa* (the very embodiment of Consciousness).

Sutra 26

पूर्वेषामपि गुरुः कालेनानवच्छेदात्

PURVESHAM API GURUH KALENA ANAVACHHEDAT.

PURVESHAM: Of the ancient forefathers. API: Also. GURUH: Preceptor. KALENA: By time. ANAVACHHEDAT: Not obstructed.

Meaning

God is the preceptor of even the ancient forefathers, and is unobstructed by time.

Explanation

Human preceptors are obstructed by time, because they must die. But the Divine Preceptor is eternal and everlasting.

Guru is one who illumines (*Ru*) the cave of the heart (*Gu*). In other words, he enables an aspirant to discover his inner, essential nature by causing the light of knowledge to shine in the depths of his *Chitta*.

The relationship between a *Guru* and his disciple is mystic. It is the Divine Self who reaches out to the disciple through the medium of a human *Guru*. The Divine Self is the cause of all Yogic movement, both within and without. Within, He promotes growing spiritual aspiration and understanding. Externally, He adopts the form of a living spiritual personality — a *Guru*.

OM illustrated.

The real *Guru* is God alone. The *Gita* and the *Upanishads* declare that the Divine Self taught even *Brahma* the Creator before the creation of the universe.

Sutra 27

तस्य वाचक: प्रणव:

TASYA VACHAKAH PRANAVAH.

TASYA: His. VACHAKA: Name. PRANAVAH: Om.

Meaning

His Name is Om.

Explanation

Om is enjoined in the *Vedas* and *Upanishads* as the most suitable sound symbol for the Divine Self. Om is the root of all *Mantras* (sacred syllables). It consists of three letters — A, U, and M, plus a nasal sound represented by a Sanskrit *Vindu* (point).

With the sound "A", one opens the mouth, and with "M", one closes the mouth. "A" is the beginning, and "M" is the closing of all that can be spoken. "U" is the connecting link denoting all that can lie between these two limits. The very chanting of a prolonged Om has a harmonious effect and is employed in *Pranayama* for harmonizing the breath and silencing the mind.

Apart from all this, Om is the symbol of the spiritual movement that leads to Self-realization. *Vedantins* (followers of the path of wisdom) meditate upon Om guided by the implications of each letter.

"A" symbolizes physical consciousness which must be resolved into astral consciousness (symbolized by "U") before a Yogi can withdraw the astral consciousness into causal consciousness (represented by "M").

Finally, having transcended the causal plane, he rises to the state of Enlightenment and discovers, "I Am That." This is denoted by the *Vindu*. Om, therefore, is described as the best support for the practice of meditation. It leads to knowledge as well as to surrender to God.

The method of repeating Om as a means to surrender to God is described in the next Sutra.

Sutra 28

तज्जपस्तदर्थभावनम्

TAT JAPAH TADARTHA BHAVANAM.

TAT JAPAH: Repetition of That (Om). TADARTHA: With its meaning. BHAVANAM: And feeling.

Meaning

Om should be repeated with meaning and feeling.

Explanation

A *Mantra* is repeated in three ways: *Vaikhari* (loudly), *Upamshu* (whispered), and *Manasic* (mentally). Mental repetition is the most effective.

However, one should not merely repeat Om without reflecting upon its meaning. Along with each repetition, he should direct his mind to God by thinking of the nature of God as described in the previous Sutras.

He should develop a *Sattwic* feeling and discover increasing sweetness by uttering the Name of God. God is the embodiment of sweetness (*Rasa Swarupa*). He is the embodiment of love (*Prema Swarupa*). He is the center, source and sustenance of this creation. He is the Inner Witness of all thoughts and feelings. He is one's true identity. These thoughts pertaining to God must be entertained while repeating Om, and this practice will gradually enable an aspirant to awaken *Mantra Chaitanya* — the mystic potency that lies hidden in each *Mantra*.

Repetition of *Mantra* fills the mind with *Sattwa* (purity). It draws divine grace to assist an aspirant on the path of Yoga. The *Gita* says, "Repetition of Om is the best of all sacrifices." *(X, 25)*

The effects of *Mantra Japa* are described in the following Sutra.

Sutra 29

ततःप्रत्यक्चेतनाधिगमोऽप्यन्तरायाभावश्च

TATAH PRATYAKCHETANA ADHIGAMOAPI ANTARAYA ABHAVASHCHA.

TATAH: By repetition of Om. PRATYAK-CHETANA: The inner Self. ADHIGAMO: Knowledge. API: Also. ANTARAYA: Obstacles. ABHAVAH: Disappearance. CHA: And.

59

Meaning

By repeating Om, obstacles are removed, and knowledge of the inner Self is acquired.

Explanation

Repetition of *Mantra* enables a person to discover increasing love of God. By surrendering to God, a Yogi begins to ascend the heights of *Samadhi*. His purified mind discovers the knowledge of his own essential nature.

He realizes that, "The Self in me is different from my body, senses, mind, intellect and ego. It is immortal, immutable and infinite. It is the *Brahman* of the *Upanishads*."

While the repetition of *Mantra* can lead one to the highest attainment, it also removes obstacles that arise on the path of Yogic movement, which are described in the following two Sutras.

Sutra 30

व्याधिस्त्यानसंशयप्रमादालस्याविरतिभ्रान्तिदर्शनालब्ध-
भूमिकत्वानवस्थितत्वानि चित्तविक्षेपास्तेऽन्तरायाः

VYADHI STYAN SAMSHAYA PRAMADA ALASYA AVIRATI BHRANTI-DARSHAN ALABDHABHUMIKATWA ANAVAS-THITATWANI CHITTAVIKSHEPAH TE ANTARAYAH.

VYADHI: Disease. STYAN: Dullness. SAMSHAYA: Doubt. PRAMADA: A procrastinating nature. ALASYA: Laziness. AVIRATI: Lack of dispassion (worldly-mindedness). BHRANTI-DARSHAN: Illusion or false knowledge. ALABDHA-

BHUMIKATWA: Inability to find any state of Yoga (missing the point). ANAVASTHITATWA: Inability to maintain a state of Yoga. CHITTAVIKSHEPAH: Distractions of the mind. TE: These are. ANTARAYAH: Obstacles.

Meaning

Disease, dullness, doubt, a procrastinating nature, laziness, lack of dispassion, false knowledge, the inability to find any state of Yoga, the inability to maintain a state of Yoga (when found), cause distractions of the mind, and are the obstacles.

Explanation

1. Disease (*Vyadhi*). Disease is of two types: *Adhi* (mental disease) and *Vyadhi* (physical disease). Mind influences the body through a network of vital channels (*Nadis*). When the *Pranas* (the vital forces) are disturbed, the humors of the body become disbalanced, resulting in a chemical disbalance in the body. This leads to various diseases.

Any defect in the body, senses or mind that restricts one's movement on the path of Yoga is a disease that needs to be treated. An aspirant should not ignore the health of his body. He should take recourse to *Hatha Yoga* exercises, *Pranayama*, proper diet, and expert help from physicians to keep his body healthy and fit.

2. Dullness (*Styan*). When one is dull, there may be willingness to progress on the path of Yoga, but there is a lack of initiative to pursue the disciplines necessary for it.

3. Doubt (*Samshaya*). This refers to doubt in one's capacity to practise Yoga, as well as in the autheticity of Yoga itself. When the mind swings between, "I will succeed in Yoga," and "I may not succeed in Yoga," it is in a state of doubt that must be overcome.

4. Procrastination (*Pramada*). The habit of postponing Yogic practices for a doubtful future constitutes *Pramada*.

5. Laziness (*Alasya*). *Tamas* causes a sense of heaviness in the mind and body. Overcome by laziness, one is not inclined to practise Yoga.

6. Worldly-mindedness (*Avirati*). If one is suffering from *Avirati*, when the senses come into contact with the objects, the mind loses its hold on *Vairagya* (dispassion). The subtle desires of the mind for the pleasures of the world have not been transfomed by the force of *Sattwa* (purity).

7. Illusion (*Bhranti-Darshan*). "This practice of Yoga is not helping me. It is harmful for me." This form of wrong knowledge is an illusion that must be overcome.

8. The inability to find any state of Yoga (*Alabdhabhumikatwa*). Due to subtle obstacles, an aspirant may be unable to discover the higher states of Yoga, such as success in meditation and experiences of *Samadhi*, in spite of his repeated effort. This discourages him on the path of Yoga.

9. Instability, or inability to maintain a state of Yoga (*Anavasthitatwa*). There are other aspirants who are able to discover a higher state of Yoga, but are unable to maintain it. It comes and goes like the passing wind.

All these obstacles are removed by successfully surrendering to God as described in Sutras 23 to 28. Another general method is given in Sutra 32. But first, along with these obstacles, there arise the following causes of mental distraction.

Sutra 31

दुःखदौर्मनस्याङ्गमेजयत्वश्वासप्रश्वासा विक्षेपसहभुवः

DUKHA DAURMANASYA ANGAMEJAYATWA SHWAS PRASHWAS VIKSHEPA SAHABHUVAH.

DUKHA: Pain. DAURMANASYA: Despair. ANGAMEJAYATWA: Shaking of the body. SHWAS: Irregular inhalation. PRASHWAS: Irregular exhalation. VIKSHEPA: Mental distraction. SAHABHUVAH: Accompany.

Meaning

Pain, despair, trembling, and irregular breathing accompany mental distractions.

Explanation

The obstacles mentioned in Sutra 30 create mental distractions. When the mind is unable to maintain a systematic form of thinking, or when it lacks the ability to focus itself on one point, it is distracted. A distracted mind attracts numerous maladies to both the mind and the body.

1. Pain (*Dukha*). There are three types of pain: (a) Subjective pain in the body or mind is caused by diseases or mental impurities such as anger, passion and greed. (b) Objective pain is caused by external sources such as thieves, snakes, or accidents. (c) Pain caused by floods, earthquakes, and similar catastrophes which are beyond human control.

2. Despair (*Daurmanasya*). Despair is a form of mental agitation caused by the frustration of desires.

3. Trembling of the body (*Angamejayatwa*). An agitated mind causes tension in the nerves, resulting in abnormal restlessness in the body. Certain limbs begin to shake and vibrate even against one's own will.

4. Irregular breathing (*Shwas Prashwas*). When the mind is restless and the body tense, one's breath becomes irregular. Breath is related to *Prana* (vital energy), and *Prana* to the mind. If the breathing is abnormal, it is difficult to bring about steadiness in the mind.

A Yogi must overcome all distractions as well as the obstacles that cause distraction by undertaking diligent methods. Apart from the supreme method of surrender to God, there is a simple, general method described in the following Sutra.

Sutra 32

तत्प्रतिषेधार्थमेकतत्त्वाभ्यासः

TAT PRATISHEDHARTHAM EKA TATTWA-BHYASAH.

TAT: Those (obstacles). PRATISHEDHARTHAM: For removing. EKA: One. TATTWA: Object of meditation. ABHYASAH: Repeated effort.

Meaning

To remove those (obstacles and mental distractions), one should repeatedly practise meditation on one object.

Explanation

Since the mind is not one-pointed, it is distracted. When the mind is allowed to come under the sway of *Rajas* and *Tamas* (the principles of distraction and darkness), it continues to intensify the negative impressions of the *Kleshas* (afflictions). Under the influence of negative thoughts and impure sentiments, one creates various obstacles on the path of Yoga.

But by repeated effort in concentration, an aspirant brings about one-pointedness in his mind. As *Sattwa* (the principle of harmony) begins to dominate the mind, there is a healthy flow of *Prana* in the body. This results in a psychophysical balance which removes numerous obstacles in one's life, and paves the way for spiritual advancement.

Instead of seeking the causes of various maladies of his mind and body, an aspirant should diligently promote the one-pointedness of his mind by taking r e c o u r s e   t o   *Abhyasa*   a n d   *Vairagya*. *(RAJA YOGA: I, 12)*

The objects of meditation are outlined in Sutras 35 to 39, and provide a broad perspective for practising one-pointedness of the mind.

The obstacles and their effects in the mind (mental distractions) are caused by subtle mental impurities known as *Mala*. A Yogi must conduct himself in his daily life with a cultured attitude in order to remove the various forms of *Mala* such as attachment, jealousy, cruelty, hatred, animosity, revengefulness, and other morbid thoughts and sentiments.

The following Sutra describes a method that can effect this removal.

Sutra 33

मैत्रीकरुणामुदितोपेक्षाणां सुखदुःखपुण्यापुण्यविषयाणां भावनातश्चित्तप्रसादनम्

MAITRI KARUNA MUDITA UPEKSHANAM SUKH DUKH PUNYA APUNYA VISHAYANAM BHAVANATASH CHITTA PRASADAM.

MAITRI: Friendliness. KARUNA: Compassion. MUDITA: Cheerfulness. UPEKSHANAM: Indifference. SUKH: Joyousness. DUKH: Afflicted with pain. PUNYA: Virtuous. APUNYA: Devoid of virtue (the sinful ones). VISHAYANAM: Objects (persons). BHAVANATASH: By mental attitude. CHITTA PRASADAM: The mind-stuff is purified.

Meaning

The mind is purified by being friendly with joyous personalities, compassionate towards the afflicted, cheerful with the virtuous, and indifferent towards the evil.

Explanation

In daily life, one encounters four types of people: those who are happy, those who are miserable, those who are virtuous, and those who are wicked and vicious. An uncultured person continues to create mental impurities by feeling attachment, hatred, jealousy, cruelty and other negative sentiments as he moves among these various types of people. But a Yogi adopts the following attitudes in order to purify his mind.

1. Friendliness towards those who are happy. By promoting the attitude of friendliness, one feels that the happiness of others is his own. Therefore, instead of being tainted by jealousy, the mind becomes vibrant with joy and a sense of magnanimity.

Further, the notion that, "I alone am entitled to happy developments," which is sustained by *Raga* (attachment), is removed, and the mind moves towards *Vairagya* (dispassion) as one begins to feel, "May all be happy."

2. Compassion towards those who are miserable. By developing compassion, one feels, "Just as I am eager to overcome the painful conditions in my life, so everyone in misery struggles for happiness and comfort."

67

The heart of a Yogi melts at the sufferings of others. He develops the good will, "May all be happy and free from afflictions." This attitude removes the common tendency to develop an insensitive heart, and thereby cruelty towards those who are afflicted.

3. Cheerfulness towards the virtuous. People often develop a form of jealousy towards those who are virtuous and spiritually advanced. They are inclined to find fault in them, because the mind has this tendency to discover faults in truly great people simply for the sake of maintaining its own negative level.

This impurity is removed by developing a sense of joyousness towards the virtuous, just as one is joyous to see his father or mother prosper and acquire fame and glory.

4. Indifference towards the wicked. When encountering people who are extremely uncultured, one can easily lose his mental balance. But an aspirant must not encourage the negative sentiments of the uncultured even in an indirect manner. By reacting to the abusive words uttered by others, one invites more abusive words. By trying to overcome the forces of evil, one becomes dominated by negative thoughts.

Therefore, it is important to maintain a rock-like indifference towards the wicked. Be deaf to their words, unconcerned when they say so many things against you, and endure their wicked acts with patience. Like thundering clouds, they will eventually dissipate before your firm indifference.

Be mentally vigilant. Do not allow the impure thoughts of anger, jealousy, hatred, animosity and pride arise in your mind. If your mind is freed from these distracting thoughts, you will discover the endless glories of the soul. And by adopting these sublime attitudes, you will become a dynamic Yogi even while you move and live in this material world.

Sutra 34

प्रच्छर्दनविधारणाभ्यां वा प्राणस्य

PRACHHARDAN VIDHARANABHYAM VA PRANASYA.

PRACHHARDAN: Exhalation of breath. **VIDHARANABHYAM:** And retention of breath. **VA:** Or. **PRANASYA:** Of the *Prana*.

Meaning

Mental purity can be attained through controlling one's *Prana* by exhalation and retention of the breath.

Explanation

The mind is linked to the body through *Pranic* functions. The *Pranas* (vital energies) flow through subtle vital channels called *Nadis*. Where these *Nadis* join, they form *Chakras* in the subtle body, and they have their corresponding seats in the spinal column. In *Kundalini Yoga*, these *Chakras* and the manner of awakening the *Kundalini Shakti* (the Cosmic *Prana* latent within) is described.

Thoughts and sentiments affect the *Pranic* system that sustains the physical body. An angry thought restricts the flow of *Prana* through the numerous *Nadis*, while a peaceful thought allows an abundance of *Prana* to flow into the body.

70 In Sukha Purvak Pranayama Pose
Author Swami Jyotir Maya Nanda

The simple method to control *Prana* that is prescribed in this Sutra is a combination of inhalation, exhalation, and retention of breath. To do this, a Yogi practises several different *Pranayama* (breathing) exercises. *(RAJA YOGA: II, 49)*

Pranayama removes the impurities of the *Nadis* and promotes purity in the mind. It produces the same results as the more psychological methods descirbed in the previous Sutra.

Next, various methods of steadying the mind are revealed.

Sutra 35

विषयवती वा प्रवृत्तिरुत्पन्ना मनसः स्थितिनिबन्धनी

VISHAYAVATI VA PRAVRITTIR UTPANNA MANASAH STHITI NIBANDHINI.

VISHAYAVATI: Pertaining to objects. VA: Or. PRAVRITTIH: The special functions of the mind. UTPANNA: Having arisen. MANASAH: Of the mind. STHITI: State. NIBANDHINI: Holds or binds.

Meaning

When the functions of the mind pertaining to divine objects arise, they bind the mind to the state of meditation (and *Samadhi*).

Explanation

As an aspirant meditates daily, *Sattwa* (purity) continues to dominate the mind. As a result of increasing purity, there arise supersensory perceptions of sight, sound, touch, taste, and smell. These supersensory perceptions, caused by the elevated functions of the mind, are called *Vishayavati Pravritti*.

A Yogi allows his mind to attain higher levels of concentration, meditation, and *Samadhi* by pursuing any supersensory perception that may arise due to the purity of his mind. This inner experience enables him to develop faith in Yoga, and perseverance in the practice of meditation. *(RAJA YOGA: III, 36)*

Sutra 36

विशोका वा ज्योतिष्मती

VISHOKA VA JYOTISHMATI.

VISHOKA: Sorrowless. VA: Or. JYOTISHMATI: Luminous.

Meaning

Or a Yogi can control his mind by pursuing that luminous function of the mind that is sorrowless.

Explanation

All Yogis do not follow the same path to the heights of meditation and *Samadhi*. Some practise *Pranayama*. Some pursue the supersensory perceptions. Some experience a luminosity in the mind that reflects the sorrowless state of the Self within. By pursuing the latter, a Yogi attains success in *Samadhi*.

LORD BUDDHA

Artist—Roberto Martinez

73

The increasing mental purity can express itself in the form of mystic lights. One may see the sun, the moon, lightning, a shining crystal, and many other forms of illumination. Lit up with the mystic light, a Yogi goes beyond all sorrows.

Sutra 37

वीतरागविषयं वा चित्तम्

VITARAGA VISHAYAM VA CHITTAM.

VITARAGA VISHAYAM: The minds of Yogis that are devoid of attachment. VA: Or. CHITTAM: Mind.

Meaning

Or by meditating upon the minds of Yogis that are devoid of attachment, one allows his mind to enter into *Samadhi*.

Explanation

By meditating upon Sages and Saints who have attained freedom from all forms of attachment, a Yogi fills his mind with *Sattwa*. This practice is seen in every religion, for devotion to Saints and Sages is considered a vital need for spiritual advancement.

A Yogi holds the example of the radiant Sages of the past and present before his mental vision. Or he adopts an ideal such as Buddha, Christ, Rama, Krishna, or any inspiring personality that leads his mind to *Samadhi*.

Sutra 38

स्वप्ननिद्राज्ञानालम्बनं वा

SWAPNA NIDRA JNANA ALAMBANAM VA.

SWAPNA: Dream. NIDRA: Sleep. JNANA:
Knowledge. ALAMBANAM: Support. VA: Or.

Meaning

Or by utilizing the support of the Yogic
knowledge of dream and sleep, a Yogi can lead his
mind to *Samadhi*.

Explanation

The study of dream and sleep includes the
waking state as well. A Yogi who meditates upon the
philosophical implication of these three states is able
to attain *Samadhi* effectively. *Jnana Yoga* (the path
of wisdom) emphasizes this form of reflective
meditation.

During the waking state, the mind is able to
contact the objects of the world. When *Rajas* (the
principle of externalization) is checked by *Tamas*
(inertia), the mind introverts. This leads to the
experience of dream.

The states of lower *Samadhi* are the positive
counterparts of dream. During dream, one operates
with the astral body, but he is unable to discover his
spiritual expansion. He is caught in the maze of his
subtle desires. But as an aspirant advances on the path
of Yoga, he controls *Rajas* by *Sattwa*, and develops a
positive internalization of the mind through lower
Samadhi. This allows him to enter into the astral
plane without any limitation or restriction caused by

The study of dream beckons the aspirant to understand the miraculous power of the mind and the state of lower *Samadhi*, wherein there is increasing freedom and joy. Also, by reflecting upon dream, a Yogi gains an insight into the fact that the world itself is a "long dream." The mind only projects the illusion of the world-process due to ignorance.

Further, sleep is brought about through increasing *Tamas*, when the mind is neither externalized nor internalized. It corresponds to the state of *Asamprajnata Samadhi* (the highest *Samadhi*). However, sleep is a negative state. But when *Rajas* is controlled by overwhelming *Sattwa*, a Yogi attains the positive counterpart of sleep by experiencing the highest form of *Samadhi*, wherein the mind has no supoort of anything external or internal.

By meditating upon the mystic implications of dream and sleep, a Yogi controls his mind and succeeds in *Samadhi*.

Also, dreams that develop on the basis of *Sattwa* give rise to many mystic experiences. A Yogi may come into contact with Divine Beings and receive initiation and encouragement from them. And such experiences are also helpful in leading a Yogi to the heights of *Samadhi*.

Sutra 39

यथाभिमतध्यानाद्वा

YATHABHIMAT DHYANAD VA.

YATHABHIMAT: According to one's choice. DHYANAT: By meditation. VA: Or.

Meaning

Or by meditating on anything of one's choice (one attains control over his mind).

Explanation

Different people have different inclinations, and Yoga does not limit one's possibilities to meditate on different objects. Whatever object is easiest to meditate upon, a Yogi should adopt for the practice of meditation. When the mind is lit up with the light of *Sattwa*, every object becomes a channel leading the Yogi to the heights of *Samadhi*.

Sutra 40

परमाणुपरममहत्त्वान्तोऽस्य वशीकार:

PARAMANU PARAMA MAHATTWANTOSYA VASHIKARAH.

PARAMANU: From the smallest, which is an atom. PARAMA MAHATTWANTAH: To the greatest, which is *Mahat Tattwa* (Cosmic Mind). ASYA: Its. VASHIKARAH: Control.

Meaning

(As a result of the practice of meditation,) the mind of a Yogi gains control over all objects, from the smallest, which is an atom, to the greatest, which is *Mahat Tattwa* (Cosmic Mind).

Explanation

As a result of repeated practice of meditation and *Samadhi*, the mind of a Yogi becomes filled with

Sattwa. Though he begins his practice of meditation on the object of his choice, as purity increases in his mind, he develops the ability to focus the mind on any object — whether it is as subtle as an atom or as vast and all-encompassing as the Cosmic Mind itself.

This point is further explained in the following Sutra.

Sutra 41

क्षीणवृत्तेरभिजातस्येव मणेर्ग्रहीतृग्रहणग्राह्येषु तत्स्थतद-ज्ञनता समापत्तिः

KSHEENA VRITTER ABHIJATASYA IVA MANER GRAHITRI GRAHANA GRAHYESHU TATSTHATADANJANATA SAMAPATTIH.

KSHEENA VRITTEH: He whose *Vrittis* (thought-waves) of the mind have become attenuated. **ABHIJATASYA:** There is born. **IVA:** Like. **MANEH:** crystal. **GRAHITRI:** Pertaining to *Mahat* (Cosmic Mind). **GRAHANA:** Pertaining to the mind and senses. **GRAHYESHU:** Pertaining to objects. **TATSTHATADANJANATA:** It (the mind) becomes steady and identified with the object of meditation. **SAMAPATTIH:** This is known as lower *Samadhi*.

Meaning

When the thought-waves are attenuated, the mind of a Yogi develops a crystal-like purity; his mind is able to focus itself as well as be identified with either *Asmita* or *Mahat*, or the subtle plane of mind and senses, or the subtle and gross objects. Then this state of the mind is called *Samapatti* or *Samprajnata Samadhi* (lower *Samadhi*).

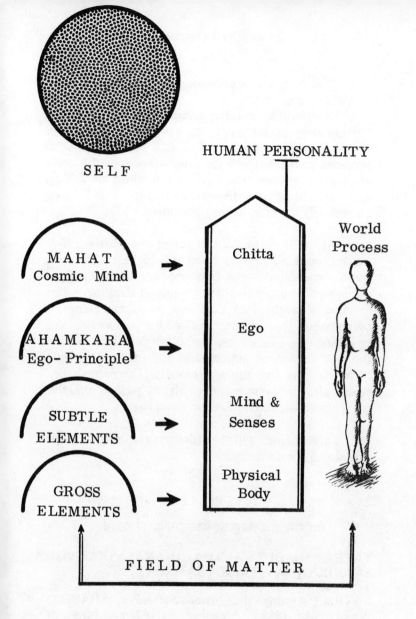

SELF

HUMAN PERSONALITY

MAHAT
Cosmic Mind

AHAMKARA
Ego- Principle

SUBTLE
ELEMENTS

GROSS
ELEMENTS

Chitta

Ego

Mind &
Senses

Physical
Body

World
Process

FIELD OF MATTER

SPIRIT & MATTER

Explanation

The purified mind is compared to a crystal. A transparent crystal becomes colored by whatever object is placed near it. If it is a rose, the crystal becomes rosy; if it is a jasmine, it assumes the color of jasmine. In the same way, the mind of a Yogi becomes identified with whatever object it is focused on through the practice of meditation.

On the basis of the categories of evolution, *Raja Yoga* groups all objects from the highest (*Mahat* or the Cosmic Mind — the first product of *Prakriti*) to the lowest atom, into three groups: 1. *Grahitri* refers to *Asmita* or the source of ego in human beings; it corresponds to *Mahat*. 2. *Grahana* comprises the ego-principle, five senses, the subtle principles behind the five organs of action, and the mind. 3. *Grahya* comprises the five subtle elements (*Tanmatras*), i.e., ether, air, fire, water and earth, as well as the five gross elements which have the same names.

This theme will be further elaborated while explaining the *Samadhis*.

Sutra 42

तत्र शब्दार्थज्ञानविकल्पैः संकीर्णा सवितर्का समापत्तिः

TATRA SHABDA ARTHA JNANA VIKALPAIH SANKIRNA SAVITARKA SAMAPATTIH.

TATRA: Among the lower *Samadhis*. SHABDA: Word. ARTHA: Meaning. JNANA: Idea or knowledge. VIKALPAIH: Imagination. SANKIRNA: Confusion. SAVITARKA: With gross plane. SAMAPATTIH: Lower *Samadhi*.

Meaning

Of the lower *Samadhis*, when there is confusion caused by imagination among word, meaning and idea, the *Samadhi* is known as *Savitarka*.

Explanation

This is the first stage of the lower *Samadhis*. The mind is able to become one with the gross object of meditation; but it is unable to go beyond some confusions that are caused by the uncontrolled function of imagination (*Vikalpa*).

For example, if an aspirant meditates upon a rose, his mind is encountering three distinct objects: 1. The grammatical English word "rose" which abides on the tongue (*Shabda*), 2. The actual rose that blooms in the garden (*Artha*), and 3. The idea of rose that abides in the mind (*Jnana*). This has already been explained in connection with Sutra 17.

In the first stage of lower *Samadhi*, a Yogi is able to develop deep meditation on a gross object, but he cannot yet go beyond the mental associations caused by name and idea pertaining to the object. When he succeeds in separating the object from all mental deviations caused by imagination, he enters into *Nirvitarka Samadhi*. This is explained in the following Sutra.

Sutra 43

स्मृतिपरिशुद्धौ स्वरूपशून्येवार्थमात्रनिर्भासा निर्वितर्का

SMRITI PARISHUDDHAU SWARUPA SHUNYEVA ARTHAMATRA NIRBHASA NIRVITARKA.

SMRITI: Memory. PARISHUDDHAU: Purification. SWARUPA SHUNYEVA: As if void of its own form. ARTHAMATRA NIRBHASA: Shining with the object alone. NIRVITARKA: *Samadhi* without confusion.

Meaning

With the purification of memory, the mind, as if devoid of itself, shines with the object alone. Then it is called *Nirvitarka Samadhi*.

Explanation

It is the uncontrolled function of memory that leads to mental imagination. It is memory that links an object with time, space, various associations and ideas. When memory is impure, it is impossible to penetrate into the object of meditation.

By attaining success in the first type of lower *Samadhi* (*Savitarka*), a Yogi is able to enter into meditation on the object without being deviated by its name and associated ideas. It is a greater and more intensive movement into the object of meditation. At this stage the mind, being pure like a crystal, becomes so colored by the object that it seems to have no existence in itself.

Sutra 44

एतयैव सविचारा निर्विचारा च सूक्ष्मविषया व्याख्याता

ETAYAIVA SAVICHARA NIRVICHARA CHA SUKSHMA VISHAYA VYAKHYATA.

ETAYAIVA: By this. SAVICHARA: *Samadhi* with reflection. NIRVICHARA: *Samadhi* without reflection. CHA: And other lower *Samadhis*. SUKSHMA VISHAYA: Pertaining to subtle objects. VYAKHYATA: Have been explained.

Meaning

By this (by the description of *Savitarka* and *Nirvitarka Samadhis*), the other *Samadhis* have been explained in the same manner.

Explanation

As *Sattwa* increases in the mind of the Yogi, he goes beyond the gross plane. The object that he adopted for the practice of meditation now becomes a channel to the subtler planes of existence.

He discovers that every object is constituted of five subtle elements, and encounters mystic experiences pertaining to these subtle elements. He may have supersensory perceptions, or see mystic lights, or hear mystic sounds, or find his mind filled with increasing joy and sublimity.

The subtle elements have their mystic colors and characteristics. *Akasha* or ether element is of blue color and is related to the *Vishudhi Chakra* at the throat. It is the source of sound. *Vayu* or air element is green in color and is related to the heart center, the *Anahata Chakra*. Perception of touch proceeds from this element.

Fire element or *Agni* has a red color, is related to the *Manipura Chakra* at the navel, and functions through sight. Water element or *Jala* is related to the

SAMADHIS AND THEIR ATTAINMENTS

SAMADHI	OBJECT OF FOCUS	ATTAINMENT
1. Savitarka & 2. Nirvitarka	Gross elements; body & gross objects; gross senses	Mastery over the gross elements; Apara Vairagya
3. Savichara & 4. Nirvichara	Subtle elements; subtle senses	Mastery over the subtle elements; Apara Vairagya; purity of mind
5. Sananda	Ahamkara or ego-principle	Gateway to many psychic powers; purity of mind
6. Asmita	Chitta or the source of the ego-principle	Viveka Khyati or Intuitive Vision; Para Vairagya
7. Asamprajnata	Withdrawal from the Chitta	Kaivalya or Liberation

Swadhishthana Chakra at the root of the generative organ, and from this element, taste arises. Earth element or *Prithwi* has a yellow color and is related to *Muladhara Chakra* (basal center); smell is its characteristic function. *Kundalini Yoga* details upon these elements and their centers.

Having passed through *Savitarka* and *Nirvitarka*, a Yogi enters the subtle plane, but is unable to separate the subtle elements from his mental associations of time, space, and other concepts. At this stage the *Samadhi* is *Savichara*. But when he rises beyond these associations, and his mind shines (identifies itself) with the subtle elements without any distortion or deviation caused by the faulty functions of memory or imagination, he attains *Nirvichara Samadhi*.

When *Nirvichara Samadhi* becomes intensified, a Yogi ascends the ladder to subtler planes of existence. He reaches the level of *Ahamkara Tattwa* (ego-principle) or the plane from which mind and senses have proceeded. Then his *Samadhi* becomes supremely joyous and is called *Sananda Samadhi*, or *Samadhi* with joy.

With increasing purity of the *Chitta* (mind-stuff), a Yogi goes beyond the ego-center and discovers the causal plane of which ego is the product. Then the *Samadhi* is called *Sasmita Samadhi* (*Samadhi* pertaining to the source of the ego — or *Samadhi* pertaining to the Cosmic Mind or *Mahat*).

The next Sutra explains the range of subtle planes of existence.

Sutra 45

सूक्ष्मविषयत्वं चालिङ्गपर्यवसानम्

SUKSHMA VISHAYATWAM CHA ALINGA PARYAVASANAM.

SUKSHMA: Subtle. **VISHAYATWAM**: Objectivity.
CHA: And. **ALINGA**: Nonmanifest (*Prakriti*).
PARYAVASANAM: The highest limit.

Meaning

Subtle objectivity extends up to the nonmanifest *Prakriti*.

Explanation

A Yogi communes with the gross objects in the first two lower *Samadhis*: *Savitarka* and *Nirvitarka*. He rises beyond the gross plane and communes with the subtler plane of elements in the next two *Samadhis*: *Savichara* and *Nirvichara*. Then he goes beyond this subtle to a yet subtler plane of the *Ahamkara Tattwa* during *Sananda Samadhi*. Having ascended still further, he enters into the cause of the ego-center, the plane of pure *Chitta* (or *Mahat*) in *Sasmita Samadhi*.

These are the six lower *Samadhis*, and they prepare a person for a mystic leap beyond the causal plane of *Prakriti* (Nature).

As a result of success in *Sasmita Samadhi*, a Yogi develops intuitive vision which reveals the Self to be distinct from the *Chitta*. This intuitive vision enables him to develop dispassion even towards the purified state of the *Chitta*. This is known as *Para Vairagya* or supreme dispassion. *(RAJA YOGA: I, 16)*

Sutra 46

ता एव सबीजः समाधिः

TA EVA SABIJAH SAMADHIH.

TA EVA: These together. SABIJAH: With seed.
SAMADHIH: Superconscious states.

Meaning

These together constitute *Samadhi* with seed.

Explanation

These six *Samprajnata Samadhis* (lower
Samadhis) need a support or basis in the form of
gross, subtle, subtler, and subtlest planes of existence.
Since they do not terminate the seed of the
world-process, they are known as *Sabija* or "with
seed," or as *Salambana* (with support).

Kaivalya or Liberation is attained by
Asamprajnata Samadhi or the highest *Samadhi*, also
called *Nirlamba* (without support) as well as *Nirbija*
(without seed).

The glorious experiences on the ascending
heights of *Samadhi* are briefly outlined in the
following Sutras.

Sutra 47

निर्विचारवैशारद्येऽध्यात्मप्रसादः

NIRVICHARA VAISHARADYA ADHYATMA
PRASADAH.

NIRVICHARA: *Nirvichara Samadhi*.
VAISHARADYA: Purification. ADHYATMA:
Intuitional knowledge. PRASADAH: Is attained.

Meaning

By the purification of *Nirvichara Samadhi*, a Yogi attains intuitional knowledge.

Explanation

As a Yogi ascends the rungs of lower *Samadhi*, his intellect becomes exceedingly purified. He develops intuitive vision, which allows him to be identified with any plane of existence. With the fullness of intuitional knowledge, he discovers the nature of the Self.

Sutra 48

ऋतम्भरा तत्र प्रज्ञा

RITAMBHARA TATRA PRAJNA.

RITA: The truth. AMBHARA: Filled. TATRA: Then. PRAJNA: Intuitive intellect.

Meaning

Then the intuitive intellect of a Yogi becomes filled with the truth.

Explanation

As a result of perfection in the lower *Samadhis*, a Yogi attains intuitive vision which reveals the Truth of the Self without a shadow of doubt and without any distortion. All illusions are dispelled by the light of intuition. The knowledge that is acquired in this state is unique, and is explained in the following Sutra.

Sutra 49

श्रुतानुमानप्रज्ञाभ्यामन्यविषया विशेषार्थत्वात्

SHRUTA ANUMAN PRAJNABHYAM ANYAVISHAYA VISHESHARTHATWAT.

SHRUTA: Heard. ANUMAN: Inference. PRAJNABHYAM: The knowledge. ANYAVISHAYA: Distinct from this knowledge. VISHESHARTHATWAT: Because of speciality.

Meaning

This knowledge is distinct from the knowledge gained by hearing (from authoritative sources) as well as from inference, because it is a specialized knowledge.

Explanation

Intuitional knowledge is different from intellectual knowledge, which is sustained by the functions of *Pramana* or right knowledge as discussed in Sutra 7.

Intellectual knowledge can be compared to the rays of the sun that illumine all objects; it is generalized. But when the rays of the sun are gathered and concentrated through a lens, there arises fire which burns. It is the specialized function of the sun.

Much in the same way, when intuition develops, there is a specialized knowledge that removes ignorance and enables one to attain Absolute Freedom from the world-process.

Sutra 50

तज्जः संस्कारोऽन्यसंस्कारप्रतिबन्धी

TAJJAH SAMSKARONYA SAMSKARA PRATIBANDHI.

TAJJAH: Born of that. SAMSKARAH: Impressions. ANYA: Other. SAMSKARA PRATIBANDHI: Remover of impressions.

Meaning

The impressions that are born of that (*Ritambhara Prajna* or intuitive intellect) bring about the removal of all impressions.

Explanation

Different types of *Samskaras* are formed according to the five different states of the mind (refer to Sutra 4 of the present chapter). All these impressions are put to an end when the sublime impressions of intuitive knowledge begins to gather in the *Chitta* of the Yogi.

Sutra 51

तस्यापि निरोधे सर्वनिरोधान्निर्बीजः समाधिः

TASYAPI NIRODHE SARVA NIRODHAT NIRBIJAH SAMADHIH.

TASYAPI: Even of that (impressions of *Ritambhara Prajna*). NIRODHE: Having been controlled. SARVA NIRODHAT: All are controlled. NIRBIJAH: Seedless. SAMADHIH: Superconsciousness.

Meaning

When even these impressions (impressions of the intuitive intellect) have been controlled, there is a total control of all impressions, and consequently there arises the seedless *Samadhi*.

Explanation

The impressions arising from the intuitive intellect are called *Nirodha Samskaras*. But even these must be overcome in order to attain supreme freedom or Liberation.

When *Sasmita Samadhi* is perfected, a Yogi develops *Viveka Khyati* or discriminative knowledge, which is the same as intuitional knowledge described by the name *Ritambhara Prajna* (truthfilled intellect). With the unfoldment of the intuitive intellect, a Yogi develops dispassion even towards the *Chitta* itself, and is known as *Para Vairagya* (supreme dispassion).

By the force of *Para Vairagya*, a Yogi promotes more *Nirodha Samskaras*, which act like fire and consume all other impressions. A Yogi then begins to experience *Niralamba Samadhi* or *Samadhi* without support, also called *Nirbija* because it puts an end to the seed of the world-process.

A Yogi determines the increase of his *Nirodha Samskaras* by experiencing the rapid decrease of the outgoing *Samskaras* of the mind. He moves from silence to boundless silence, from peace to unfathomable peace, from fullness to boundless fullness.

Just as a fire is extinguished after it has consumed its fuel, so the *Nirodha Samskaras* are extinguished (or controlled) when all outgoing impressions are removed. This is the state of Liberation, described as *Kaivalya*. *(RAJA YOGA: III, 50)*

The *Chitta* exists for two purposes: *Bhoga* — to give enjoyments to the soul, and *Apavarga* — to give Liberation from the fetters of Karmas and from the cycles of birth and death. When a Yogi attains the twofold purpose of the *Chitta*, his *Chitta* then returns to its source — *Prakriti* or Nature.

A Yogi attains Liberation during his life (*Jivanmukti*). When the *Prarabdha* Karma (Karma that sustains the present body) is exhausted, he leaves the body and attains disembodied Liberation (*Videhamukti*).

Thus ends the first chapter
known as Samadhi Pad
in the Raja Yoga of Patanjali Maharshi.

*See YOGA WISDOM OF THE UPANISHADS
by Swami Jyotir Maya Nanda

CHAPTER 2 – SADHANA PAD

In the first chapter it has been explained that Yoga is the cessation of the thought-waves of the mind. The classifications of thought-waves and the various methods of controlling them have been described for advanced aspirants. Among the methods of promoting *Samadhi*, the highest are *Abhyasa* (repeated practice), *Vairagya* (dispassion) and *Ishwar Pranidhana* (surrender to God).

In this chapter, *Raja Yoga* details upon the removal of mental impurities in order to prepare the field of the *Chitta* (mind-stuff) for the advanced practice of meditation and *Samadhi*. The very first Sutra commences with the technique of purifying the *Chitta*, known as *Kriya Yoga* (the Yoga of purification).

Sutra 1

तपःस्वाध्यायेश्वरप्रणिधानानि क्रियायोगः

TAPAH SWADHYAYA ISHWAR PRANIDHANANI KRIYA YOGAH.

TAPAH: Austerity. **SWADHYAYA:** Study of scriptures and repetition of *Mantra*. **ISHWAR PRANIDHANANI:** Surrender to God. **KRIYA YOGAH:** Yoga of purification.

Meaning

Austerity, Study of scriptures and Surrender to God constitute *Kriya Yoga*, the Yoga of purifying the mind.

Explanation

These three methods fall under the category of the *Niyamas* or the observances described in Sutra 32 of this chapter. Because of their effectiveness in purifying the mind, they are mentioned in the beginning of this chapter.

Tapa or austerity consists in performing one's duties with patience, undergoing physical and mental ailments with endurance and forbearance, and observing fasts and other intensive forms of spiritual disciplines. An aspirant should develop a spirit of austerity towards all painful conditions in life, such as parting from dear relatives, loss in business, sickness, age, death, and other calamities. Just as gold is purified by subjecting it to fire, in the same way, austerity promotes golden purity in the mind.

Swadhyaya refers not only to the study of scripture, but also to the repetition of *Mantra*. Daily study of *Srimad Bhagavad Gita*, the *Upanishads*, and numerous other texts of Yoga and Vedanta philosophy offers an effective form of *Satsanga* or good association to the aspirant. One should study with profound devotion under the guidance of a spiritual preceptor, and should practise reflection and meditation in order to gain insight into the meaning of the scriptures. Scriptures also reveal their secrets to one devoted to his *Guru* and to God.

Ishwar Pranidhana or surrender to God implies adopting the attitude of being an instrument in the divine hands. An aspirant should practise the path of devotion by listening to the glory of God, singing His divine praises, repeating the divine *Mantras*, and serving Him through humanity. He should gradually bring about the surrender of his entire personality to God through increasing divine love. Surrender to God leads to *Samadhi* or superconsciousness. *(RAJA YOGA: I, 23)*

The effects as well as the purpose of *Kriya Yoga* are described in the following Sutra.

Sutra 2

समाधिभावनार्थः क्लेशतनूकरणार्थश्च

SAMADHI BHAVANA ARTHAH KLESHA TANU KARANARTHASHCHA.

SAMADHI: Superconsciousness. BHAVANA ARTHAH: For the success in. KLESHA: Afflictions. TANU: Attenuation. KARANARTHAH: The cause of. CHA: And.

Meaning

This *Kriya Yoga* is the cause of attaining success in *Samadhi* and in destroying the *Kleshas* (afflictions).

Explanation

A Yogi reduces the *Kleshas* by the practice of *Kriya Yoga*. This promotes success in *Samadhi* which leads to intuitional knowledge. As a result of intuitional knowledge, ignorance is removed and the process of destruction of the *Kleshas* is completed. *Kriya Yoga* must, therefore, be practised regularly with intensity and devotion; it is the key to spiritual advancement. *Samadhi* and its fruits have been described in the first chapter. The *Kleshas* are now being described in the following Sutras.

Sutra 3

अविद्यास्मितारागद्वेषाभिनिवेशाः क्लेशाः

AVIDYA ASMITA RAGA DWESHA ABHINIVESHAH KLESHAH.

AVIDYA: Ignorance. **ASMITA:** Egoism. **RAGA:** Attachment. **DWESHA:** Hatred. **ABHINIVESHAH:** Fear of death or clinging to life. **KLESHAH:** Afflictions.

Meaning

These are the afflictions: Ignorance, Egoism, Attachment, Hatred, and Clinging to life (or Fear of death).

Explanation

These five are the basis of all sufferings. Their impressions are called *Klishta Samskaras* or impressions that give rise to suffering and sorrow. More details about these are given in the following Sutras.

Sutra 4

अविद्या क्षेत्रमुत्तरेषां प्रसुप्ततनुविच्छिन्नोदाराणाम्

AVIDYA KSHETRAM UTTARESHAM PRASUPTA TANU VICHHINNA UDARANAM.

AVIDYA: Ignorance. **KSHETRAM:** Field. **UTTARESHAM:** The afflictions that follow ignorance. **PRASUPTA:** Dormant. **TANU:** Attenuated. **VICHHINNA:** Overpowered. **UDARANAM:** Fully expanded.

Meaning

With Ignorance as the field (source), the afflictions exist in these (four) states: Dormant, Attenuated, Overpowered, and Fully expanded.

Explanation

Ignorance is the source of these afflictions: egoism, attachment, hatred, and clinging to life. They exist in the dormant state (*Prasupta*) in children, for, one notices that as the children grow, the afflictions slowly begin to appear. They also exist in the dormant state during sleep and during *Pralaya* (cosmic involution).

In Yogis who have practised *Kriya Yoga* and who have advanced on the path of meditation and *Samadhi*, the *Kleshas* are attenuated, but their root (ignorance) has not yet been removed. If the spiritual *Sadhana* (discipline) is slackened, the mind which is apparently pure and tranquil will soon be overcome by the *Kleshas* and their numerous ramifications.

In most people the *Kleshas* exist in the *Vichhinna* or overpowered state (i.e., one form of impression is suppressed by another opposing form of impression). When a person is in a loving mood, the impressions of hatred exist in this overpowered state, and during the mood of hatred, the impressions of love are in the overpowered state. When love is kindled, all good qualities of a person are remembered, but when hatred dominates, all negative points are recalled by the mind. So, while hating, love continues to exist; while loving, hatred continues to lurk.

When the afflictions operate without any restriction, they are called *Udara* or expanded. When one feels tender sentiments towards a friend, the affliction of *Raga* or attachment is in the expanded state, while the affliction of *Dwesha* or hatred is in the overpowered state.

By the practice of Yogic *Sadhana*, one brings about the attenuated state of the *Kleshas*. It is only during the highest form of *Samadhi* that the veil of ignorance is removed and the *Kleshas* are completely destroyed through the fire of knowledge. And this state, termed *Dagdha Avistha* or the burnt up state, exists only in Liberated Sages.

The *Kleshas* are now being defined.

Sutra 5

अनित्याशुचिदुःखानात्मसु नित्यशुचिसुखात्मख्यातिरविद्या

ANITYA ASHUCHI DUHKHANAM ANATMASU NITYA SHUCHI SUKHA ATMAKHYATIR AVIDYA.

ANITYA: Non-eternal. ASHUCHI: Impure. DUHKHANAM: Pain. ANATMASU: Not-self. NITYA: Eternal. SHUCHI: Pure. SUKHA: Happiness. ATMAKHYATIH: The experience of selfhood. AVIDYA: Ignorance.

Meaning

Ignorance consists of taking the non-eternal to be the eternal, the impure to be the pure, the painful to be the pleasant, and the not-self to be the Self.

Explanation

Avidya or ignorance abides in the causal body of a person. It is sustained by a trace of *Tamas* (inertia) that exists in the *Chitta* (mind-stuff) which is a product of the three *Gunas*. It is *Avidya* that distorts the vision of the Self, thereby bringing about a limited awareness of individuality whirling through the cycles of birth and death, and subject to the bondage of desires, actions and their fructifications. This distorted vision is explained in this Sutra.

The world is non-eternal, but it is because of ignorance that it is taken to be the eternal residence for the soul. The impure body is constituted of flesh, blood, and various other rotting materials, but again, due to ignorance, it is taken to be the pure Self. Also, the enjoyments of the senses lead to the development of numerous miseries, but, in spite of this fact, they are considered the source of joy and happiness. *(RAJA YOGA: II, 15)*

The *Pranas* (vital forces), body, mind, senses, intellect, and ego all belong to the category of the not-self. But due to the mystic veil of ignorance, the spirit in man becomes identified with this not-self.

This distorted vision is not to be confused with *Viparyaya Vritti* (wrong knowledge) described in Sutra 8 of the first chapter. *Viparyaya* concerns the knowledge of objects and can be corrected through right perception, while *Avidya* is the mystic ignorance and can be removed only by the intuitional realization of the Self.

The next *Klesha*, *Asmita* or egoism, is now described.

Sutra 6

दृग्दर्शनशक्त्योरेकात्मतेवास्मिता

DRIG DARSHAN SHAKTYOR EKATMATA IVA ASMITA.

DRIG: Seer. DARSHAN: Seeing. SHAKTYOH: Power. EKATMATA: Oneness. IVA: In appearance. ASMITA: Egoism.

Meaning

Egoism consists of the apparent oneness between the power of the seer (the Self or *Purusha*) and the power of the Seen (*Prakriti* or Nature in the form of *Chitta*).

Explanation

It has been explained in the previous Sutra that due to ignorance the *Chitta*, which belongs to the not-self, is taken to be the Self. As a result of this, the power of the Self, which has the nature of eternal freedom, immutability and transcendence, is confused with the power of the *Chitta* which expresses itself through the changing *Gunas* (modes of Nature). This confusion results in *Asmita* or egoism. *Asmita* is responsible for creating these erroneous notions: "I am happy. I am miserable. I am healthy and handsome. I am unhealthy and deprived of good looks." *Asmita*, then, gives rise to the *Kleshas* explained in the next three Sutras.

Sutra 7

सुखानुशयी रागः

SUKHANUSHAYI RAGAH.

SUKHA: Happiness. ANUSHAYI: That which follows. RAGAH: Attachment.

Meaning

Attachment is that which follows happiness.

Explanation

Identified with the limited mind, one becomes dominated by an egoistic vision of life, and is thereby compelled to seek pleasure from the objects of the world. Whenever one enjoys an object or experiences happiness in any form, he develops a subtle will to have the object again and again, or to experience this happiness more and more. This becomes the basis for the formation of the impressions known as *Raga Klesha* — the affliction of attachment.

Sutra 8

दुःखानुशयी द्वेषः

DUHKHANUSHAYI DWESHAH.

DUHKHA: Pain. ANUSHAYI: That which follows. DWESHAH: Hatred.

Meaning

Hatred is that which follows pain.

Explanation

In the same way, whenever one experiences pain, a subtle will develops in the mind to be free from the pain or to remove the object that obstructs the experience of happiness. This causes the formation of impressions known as *Dwesha Klesha* — the affliction of hatred.

Sutra 9

स्वरसवाही विदुषोऽपि तथारूढोऽभिनिवेशः

SWARASVAHI VIDUSHOPI TATHARUDHO ABHINIVESHAH.

SWARASVAHI: Flowing with spontaneity (from past lives). VIDUSHOPI: Even the learned. TATHARUDHO: Present (in the learned) in the same way as in the dull-witted. ABHINIVESHAH: Clinging to life.

Meaning

Abhinivesha Klesha, the affliction of clinging to life, exists equally in the learned as in the dull-witted, since it flows with spontaneity (from past lives).

Explanation

The formation of impressions caused by attachment and hatred becomes the basis for the performance of selfish actions (*Sakamya Karmas*) which give rise to embodiment. The spirit is born again and again due to the Karmas of the past, and since ignorance is beginningless, the soul has been experiencing repeated cycles of birth and death from beginningless time.

In every embodiment, one becomes attached to life and dreads death. During the time of death, the mind generates impressions of fear of death and craving for life. These impressions cause *Abhinivesha Klesha*, or clinging to life.

Both the ignorant and the learned scholars are equally concerned about their life, and they react equally through fear to any situation that threatens their life. *Abhinivesha* literally means "that which has entered deep," and is so called because of its deep-rooted nature.

Thus, the five *Kleshas* or afflictions are: *Avidya* (ignorance), *Asmita* (egoism), *Raga* (attachment), *Dwesha* (hatred), and *Abhinivesha* (clinging to life or fear of death). These same *Kleshas* are given different names in the *Samkhya* school of philosophy, and are respectively called: *Tamas* (darkness), *Moha* (delusion), *Mahamoha* (great delusion), *Tamisra* (great darkness), and *Andha Tamisra* (intense darkness).

Sutra 10

ते प्रतिप्रसवहेयाः सूक्ष्माः

TE PRATIPRASAVA HEYAH SUKSHMAH.

TE: They. PRATIPRASAVA: By the method of resolving the *Chitta* back to its cause. HEYAH: Are to be abandoned. SUKSHMAH: In their subtle form.

Meaning

Having brought the *Kleshas* to their subtle form, they are to be destroyed (abandoned) by resolving the *Chitta* back into its source (cause).

Explanation

It has been explained in Sutra 2 that *Kriya Yoga* (the purificatory Yoga consisting of austerity, study of scriptures, and surrender to God) reduces the *Kleshas* into their subtle form. In this subtle state, the root of the *Kleshas*, *Avidya*, continues to exist. Therefore, a Yogi must ascend the ladder of *Samadhi* (superconsciousness) until he attains *Viveka Khyati* or intuitive vision. Led by this intuitive vision, the Yogi renounces the very *Chitta* itself and allows it to return to its source, *Prakriti*. In this way the *Kleshas* are completely eradicated.

Sutra 11

ध्यानहेयास्तद्वृत्तयः

DHYAN HEYAH TAD VRITTAYAH.

DHYAN: Meditation. HEYAH: To be abandoned. TAD: Their. VRITTAYAH: Functions.

Meaning

The *Kleshas*, along with their functions, are to be abandoned (or controlled) by the practice of meditation.

Explanation

A Yogi must keep a constant watch over his mind, for the *Kleshas* continue to create impure and gross thought-waves that operate in the conscious plane of the mind. They create thoughts of joy, sorrow, hate, fear, anger, passion, and other manifold forms of illusion. They are to be controlled by repeatedly directing the mind to the object of meditation.

In brief, the above Sutras have enjoined the following practices in succession: 1. The practice of *Kriya Yoga* as described in the first Sutra, thereby purifying the deeper parts of the mind. 2. The practice of meditation, bringing about the control of the effects of the *Kleshas* operating at the conscious plane of the mind. 3. Gradually bringing about the attenuated state of the *Kleshas*. 4. Ascending the heights of *Samadhi*, thereby burning down the root of the *Kleshas*, ignorance, by the fire of wisdom.

Why the *Kleshas* should be abandoned or destroyed is explained in the following Sutras.

Sutra 12

क्लेशमूल: कर्माशयो दृष्टादृष्टजन्मवेदनीय: २-१२

KLESHA MULAH KARMASHAYO DRISHTA ADRISHTA JANMA VEDANIYAH.

KLESHA: Afflictions. MULAH: The root. KARMASHAYO: The receptacle of Karma (the Karmic impressions). DRISHTA: The seen (of this birth). ADRISHTA: The unseen (of births to come). JANMA VEDANIYAH: Are to be experienced in different births.

Meaning

With the *Kleshas* as the root, the Karmic impressions give rise to fruits (of pleasure and pain) that are to be enjoyed in the present birth as well as in future births.

Explanation

As long as *Kleshas* exist in the *Chitta* (mind-stuff), so long the soul must continue to revolve in the cycles of birth and death to experience the fructification of Karmas.

The *Kleshas* are at the root of the Karmic involvements of the soul. It is because of the presence of the *Kleshas* that a person performs *Sakamya Karmas* (actions with selfish desire), thereby creating the subtle potency for future experiences of pleasure and pain.

The visible world in the present birth, as well as the unseen worlds in future births, are in store for the soul because of its Karmic involvements. Therefore, the *Kleshas* must be destroyed in order to attain Liberation.

Sutra 13

सति मूले तद्विपाको जात्यायुर्भोगाः

SATI MULE TADVIPAKO JATYAYURBHOGAH.

SATI MULE: While the root is there. TADVIPAKO: The receptacle of Karma brings forth. JATI: Class. AYUH: Life. BHOGAH: Enjoyments.

Meaning

While the root is there, the receptacle of Karma brings forth class, life, and enjoyment.

Explanation

As long as the *Kleshas* exist, the soul is bound to the fructification of Karmas. For simplicity, Karma is of three types: 1. *Sanchita* — accumulated store of Karmas from many past embodiments, 2. *Prarabdha* — fructifying Karma (only a portion of Karma from the accumulated store that becomes the basis of the present embodiment), and 3. *Kriyamana* — the actions that are being generated day by day, which will either join the *Prarabdha* and become operative in this very life, or join the *Sanchita* and become operative in future lives.

Karmic fructification determines the following:

Jati (the class in which one is born). The soul can be born in subhuman levels of living beings such as birds and animals, or it can be born in human and superhuman levels. And even while entering into human embodiment, the soul, led by its Karma, goes to different families: rich or poor, virtuous or sinful, highly elevated or sunk in illusions.

Ayu (life). The duration of life is determined by the fructifying Karma of the past. However, a certain degree of alteration can be made by one's present effort in the form of practising *Asana, Pranayama*, and various other Yogic disciplines for prolonging life. Contrariwise, lack of self-effort can reduce one's life period.

Bhoga (enjoyment). Experiences of pleasure and pain are called *Bhoga*,* and in every embodiment

---

* *Bhoga literally means enjoyment, but implies experience of pleasure and pain as a result of Karmic fructification, as well as experiences arising out of lower Samadhi.*

such experiences continue to alternate. Animals, birds, insects and all subhuman levels of existence are called *Bhoga Yoni* — embodiments meant for enjoying (experiencing) Karmas of the past, and in such embodiments, no new Karmas can be formed.

Human embodiment, however, is a rare opportunity for the soul, for *Purushartha* or self-effort is possible. A human being can modify the Karmic fructifications of the past by his present efforts; he can reduce the negative Karmas of the past, enrich the positive ones, and by the practice of Yoga, he can bring about the eradication of the very root of the Karmic tree. He can attain Self-realization and become free from the world-process even in his present life.

Sutra 14

ते ह्लादपरितापफलाः पुण्यापुण्यहेतुत्वात्

TE HLAD PARITAPA PHALAH PUNYA APUNYA HETUTWAT.

TE: They. HLAD: Joy (pleasure). PARITAPA: Sorrow (pain). PHALAH: Fruits. PUNYA: Virtue. APUNYA: Vice. HETUTWAT: Because of.

Meaning

They (class, life, and enjoyment) give rise to the fruits of pleasure and pain because of virtue and vice.

Explanation

When virtuous Karmas fructify, *Sattwa* or purity increases in one's nature. This brings about expansion in one's consciousness, resulting in the feeling of joyousness. But when vicious Karmas fructify, *Rajas* (distraction) and *Tamas* (inertia) increase at the expense of *Sattwa*, resulting in the contraction of one's consciousness. This gives rise to experiences of bitterness, pain, misery and sorrow.

A normal person endeavors to prevent pain and to promote happiness in his life. By gaining an insight into the law of Karma, he should not perform Karmas that are negative and sinful, but should perform good deeds, thereby enriching his Karmic treasure, which is the basis for future happiness. However, since good and evil are relative terms, it is difficult for a person to ward off all negative Karmas. This being so, a wise man understands that even positive Karmas are to be ultimately transcended, because their fruits are perishable, and furthermore, what seems to be pleasant is, in reality, pain in disguise.

In brief, while a person must endeavor to perform good deeds, he must also gain an insight into the art of going beyond good and evil. This is done by rooting out the *Kleshas*, thereby allowing one to attain Liberation. This point is elaborated in the following Sutra.

Sutra 15

परिणामतापसंस्कारदुःखैर्गुणवृत्तिविरोधाच्च दुःखमेव सर्वं विवेकिनः

PARINAM TAP SAMSKAR DUHKHAIH GUNA-VRITTI VIRODHAT CHA DUHKHAM EVA SARVAM VIVEKINAH.

PARINAM: Consequences. TAP: Feverish effort. SAMSKAR: Impressions. DUHKHAIH: Pain. GUNA-VRITTI: Functions of the modes of Nature.

VIRODHAT: Their mutual contradictory nature.
CHA: Also. DUHKHAM: Pain. EVA: Indeed.
SARVAM: All. VIVEKINAH: For the wise.

Meaning

Misery is implied in all pleasures because of the consequence, feverish effort, and formation of impressions, and also because of the mutual conflict that exists among the modes of Nature. Thus, all pleasures are indeed painful for the wise.

Explanation

Just as dust particles that settle on the body do not give rise to discomfort, but when they come in contact with the sensitive eyes bring immeditate pain, in the same way, while the mind of the masses is insensitive to the perception of pain in pleasant circumstances, the sensitive mind of a wise man sees pleasure as nothing but pain masquerading itself in alluring colors. The following points give insight into this truth:

1. *Parinam Duhkha* — perception of misery by reflecting upon the consequences of pleasure. Sense-enjoyments rob one of vitality and energy. Though pleasant like nectar in the beginning, they prove to be like poison in the end. *Parinam* also refers to continuing changes that occur in the objects of the world. Youth gives way to old age, and all objects of pleasure continue to change and are ultimately perishable.

2. *Tapa Duhkha* — perception of misery due to feverish effort involved in securing pleasure. With great longing and effort a person tries to secure the

objects of his desire. Then while enjoying the object, the person is concerned as to how to keep the object in his possession by warding off any obstacle that might threated its security.

For example, there is much effort involved in acquiring wealth, there is much effort in protecting it from robbers, thieves and swindlers, and there is intense pain when the wealth is lost. By reflecting on the trouble and pain involved in securing objects of such illusory pleasure, one begins to aspire for attaining Self-realization, like *Nachiketa* in the *Kathopanishad*.

3. *Samskara Duhkha* — perception of misery due to the formation of impressions. Every experience of sense-enjoyment creates impressions of attachment in the mind. Along with such impressions, further impressions of hatred, bitterness, jealousy, fear and infatuation develop. Therefore, when any object of pleasure is lost, or when a dear relative has departed, a person grieves through the memories of past joys.

4. *Guna Vritti Virodha* — perception of misery by seeing the contradictory nature of the *Gunas* (modes of Nature). When *Sattwa* (purity) arises, one is inclined to serenity, inward reflection, and derives joy through the study of scriptures, good association and the performance of good Karmas. But when *Rajas* (activity) arises, one is inclined to pursue the objects of the senses and experiences increasing tension and distraction of the mind. When *Tamas* (inertia) manifests, one is inclined to passivity, dullness, and ignorance, making the objects that seemed delightful during *Rajas* lose their charm.

The same object that is delightful and needed in one state of mind becomes despicable in another. As the *Gunas* continue to change, the mind continues to pass through its different moods. By thus reflecting, a wise man is not deluded by the apparent pleasures of the senses.

A *Sattwic* (joyous) state of mind is constantly threatened by the emergence of *Rajas* and *Tamas* from one's unconscious. While a person is immersed in *Sattwa*, there is always a subtle undercurrent feeling of fear and pathos caused by the awareness of the fact that the lower *Gunas* are waiting the express themselves.

Having examined the pleasures of the world in this manner, an aspirant should develop *Vairagya* or dispassion. He should endeavor to rise above virtue and vice by rooting out the tree of Karma and by eradicating the *Kleshas* as already described.

The following Sutras focus upon a philosophical insight into pain in order to bring about its cessation.

Sutra 16

हेयं दुःखमनागतम्

HEYAM DUHKHAM ANAGATAM.

HEYAM: Fit to be abandoned. DUHKHAM: Pain. ANAGATAM: That which has not yet come.

Meaning

Pain that has not yet come is fit to be abandoned.

Explanation

Pain that has already been experienced in the past does not merit any consideration. But pain that is to come can be avoided, removed, and destroyed.

When a physician studies a disease, he considers four points: 1. The diagnosis or the nature of the disease, 2. The cause of the disease, 3. The method of removing the disease, and 4. The prognosis or the state of health anticipated after the disease has been removed. Following this example, Sage *Patanjali Maharshi* (who is also believed to have been an authority in the Indian medical system) also describes four points: 1. The nature of pain that is to be abandoned (*Heya*), 2. The cause of pain (*Heya Hetu*), 3. The method of removing pain (*Heyopaya*), and 4. The cessation of pain (*Hana*).

Heya has already been described, and the next Sutra discusses the nature of *Heya Hetu* — the cause of pain.

Sutra 17

द्रष्टृदृश्ययोः संयोगो हेयहेतुः

DRISTRI DRISHYAYOH SAMYOGO HEYA HETUH.

DRISTRI: Seer. DRISHYAYOH: Seen. SAMYOGO: Contact. HEYA HETUH: The cause of pain (to be abandoned).

Meaning

The contact between Seer and seen is the cause of pain (to be abandoned).

Explanation

The seer is the Self which is of the nature of pure consciousness. The seen is Nature or *Prakriti* which manifests in the form of the *Chitta* or the mind-stuff. By the force of ignorance (*Avidya*), there develops a contact (*Samyoga*) between seer and seen, i.e., they are identified with each other. This is a strange blend of consciousness and matter (the Self and the mind-stuff) which is the cause of pain. The following Sutras explain the three terms seer, seen, and contact.

Sutra 18

प्रकाशक्रियास्थितिशीलं भूतेन्द्रियात्मकं भोगापवर्गार्थं दृश्यम्

PRAKASH KRIYA STHITI SHILAM BHUTA INDRIYA ATMAKAM BHOGA APAVARGARTHAM DRISHYAM.

PRAKASH: Light. **KRIYA**: Activity. **STHITI**: Inertia. **SHILAM**: Nature. **BHUTA**: Elements. **INDRIYA**: Senses. **ATMAKAM**: Consists of. **BHOGA**: Enjoyment. **APAVARGA**: Liberation. **ARTHAM**: Purpose. **DRISHYAM**: The seen.

Meaning

The seen is of the nature of light (*Sattwa*), activity (*Rajas*), and inertia (*Tamas*), and consists of the elements and the senses. It exists for the purpose of giving enjoyment and Liberation (to the soul).

Explanation

According to Yogic philosophy, *Prakriti* or Nature is the material cause of creation, and consists of a balance between the three *Gunas* — *Sattwa*,

Rajas, and Tamas. Sattwa is the principle of luminosity and wisdom; Rajas is the principle of activity and passion; and Tamas is the principle of inertia and darkness. These three Gunas go to form all the planes of the material creation — Mahat (Cosmic Mind), Ahamkara (ego-principle), Indriyas (mind, 5 subtle senses, 5 subtle organs of action), the subtle elements, the gross elements, and the physical bodies of all living beings.

The elements and the senses are mentioned because of their prominence in human existence. They indicate, in fact, the entire range of material evolution, beginning with Prakriti and ending with the gross elements, and this field of matter is called Drishya (the seen).

The seen exists for the purpose of giving Bhoga (enjoyment or experience) and Apavarga (Liberation) to the soul. The term Bhoga includes both the experiences of pleasure and pain brought about by Karmas and by the experiences of the lower Samadhis. After the soul has evolved through various experiences of pleasure and pain, it turns its steps to the ascending heights of Yoga where it enjoys the increasing delights of Samadhi.

These experiences in turn allow the soul to develop Para Vairagya or supreme dispassion, where it then turns away from the very Chitta itself. So the very same Prakriti (or Nature, or the seen) that has involved the soul in matter now promotes the withdrawal of the soul from the bondage of matter, enabling it to enter into Asamprajnata Samadhi, the highest state of superconsciousness wherein it is liberated from the cycles of birth and death. This is known as Apavarga.

EVOLUTION CHART

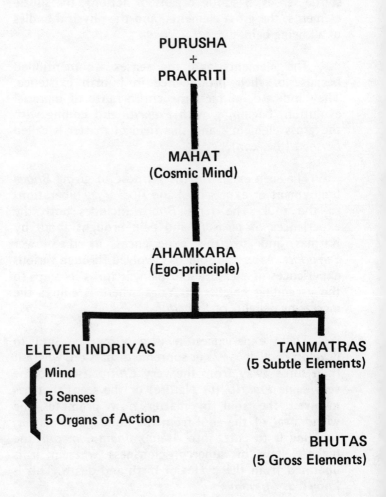

PURUSHA
+
PRAKRITI

MAHAT
(Cosmic Mind)

AHAMKARA
(Ego-principle)

ELEVEN INDRIYAS

Mind

5 Senses

5 Organs of Action

TANMATRAS
(5 Subtle Elements)

BHUTAS
(5 Gross Elements)

The world-process that every soul encounters is never without a purpose. Nature does not unfold conditions in life in a chaotic manner. The divine purpose of leading the soul to the awareness of its intrinsic reality, the Self, is implicit in Nature and all her evolutes.

Sutra 19

विशेषाविशेषलिङ्गमात्रालिङ्गानि गुणपर्वाणि

VISHESHA AVISHESHA LINGAMATRA ALINGANI GUNAPARVANI.

VISHESHA: Defined. AVISHESHA: Undefined. LINGAMATRA: With Mark. ALINGANI: Without Mark. GUNAPARVANI: The stages of the modes of Nature.

Meaning

These are the stages of the modes of Nature: Defined, Undefined, With Mark, and Without Mark.

Explanation

The 24 *Tattwas* (principles constituting cosmic evolution fall into these four categories:

1. Defined — five gross elements, five senses, five organs of action, and mind.

2. Undefined — five subtle elements and the ego-principle.

3. With Mark — Cosmic Mind (*Mahat Tattwa*). This is the mark of commencement of the evolutionary process.

4. Without Mark — Nature (*Prakriti*). Since Nature is the balance of the three *Gunas*, and since it is without any differentiation or manifestation, it is called Without Mark.

Thus the 24 *Tattwas* constitute *Drishya*, the seen, or the world of experience for every soul.

The following Sutra describes the nature of the seer.

Sutra 20

द्रष्टा दृशिमात्रः शुद्धोऽपि प्रत्ययानुपश्यः

DRISHTA DRISHI MATRAH SHUDDHOPI PRATYAYA-ANUPASHYAH.

DRISHTA: The Seer. DRISHI MATRAH: Pure consciousness. SHUDDHAH API: Though pure. PRATYAYA-ANUPASHYAH: Follows the thought-waves of the *Chitta* through identification.

Meaning

The Seer is pure consciousness, but though pure, it follows the thought-waves of the *Chitta* through identification.

Explanation

The Seer or the Self is of the nature of pure consciousness. It is immutable, changeless, associationless and free from afflictions.

As long as the Seer is dominated by ignorance, so long it continues to become identified with the thought-waves of the mind. But when ignorance is destroyed by intuitional knowledge, the Seer discovers its essential nature and is no longer associated with the seen. Then without the seen, it ceases to be the Seer.

The following Sutra emphasizes the fact that the seen exists for the Seer only.

Sutra 21

तदर्थ एव दृश्यस्याऽऽत्मा

TADARTHA EVA DRISHYASYA ATMA.

TADARTHA: For the purpose of that (the Seer). **EVA:** Alone. **DRISHYASYA:** Of the seen. **ATMA:** Nature.

Meaning

The nature of the seen exists for the purpose of the Seer alone.

Explanation

This Sutra reemphasizes what has been explained in Sutra 18. The entire world-process exists for serving the soul. Matter has no existence or reality without consciousness, and it is consciousness that lends reality to it. Matter cannot be known to exist without consciousness, and if consciousness is taken away from matter, it will cease to exist.

Sutra 22

कृतार्थं प्रति नष्टमप्यनष्टं तदन्यसाधारणत्वात्

KRITARTHAM PRATI NASHTAM APYANASHTAM TADANYA SADHARANATWAT.

KRITARTHAM PRATI: For the soul that attained Liberation. NASHTAM: Destroyed. API: Yet (this Nature). ANASHTAM: Not destroyed. TAT: That. ANYA SADHARANATWAT: Because it is common to others.

Meaning

Though destroyed for him who has attained Liberation, *Prakriti* is not yet destroyed for others because it is common to them.

Explanation

Prakriti (Nature) is the common property of all souls. While souls that attain Liberation no longer have any need for *Prakriti*, others that are not yet liberated need the sustenance of *Prakriti* for spiritual evolution and ultimate freedom.

According to *Raja Yoga* philosophy, *Prakriti* is beginningless and eternal, and it is said to be destroyed when the soul is liberated, because it is no longer needed. But, according to Vedantic philosophy, *Prakriti* is illusory, and the intuitive vision of a Sage tears this veil of illusion by seeing *Brahman* or the Absolute as the non-dual Reality. Just as in the illusion of seeing a snake in a rope, the snake vanishes when light is brought, in the same way *Prakriti* vanishes when *Brahman* is realized. These differences in philosophical views are maintained to help aspirants in their different levels of evolution.

Sutra 23

स्वस्वामिशक्त्योः स्वरूपोपलब्धिहेतुः संयोगः

SWASWAMI SHAKTYOH SWARUPA UPALABDHI HETUH SAMYOGAH.

SWA: Its own power (*Prakriti*). SWAMI SHAKTI: The power of the Lord (*Purusha*). SWARUPA: Nature. UPALABDHI: Recognition. HETUH: Cause. SAMYOGAH: Contact.

Meaning

Contact is meant for discovering the power of its own (Nature or *Prakriti*), and the power of the Lord (Spirit or *Purusha*).

Explanation

In Sutra 17, three terms were introduced for understanding the cause of pain: seer, seen, and contact. Seer or *Drashta* was explained in Sutra 20, and seen or *Drishya* was explained in Sutras 21 and 22. The third term, contact or *Samyoga*, is now being explained.

Purusha is the detached seer and is associated with *Prakriti* in order to gain the knowledge of both the power of *Prakriti* and the power of the Lord of *Prakriti*, the Self. When the seer is identified with the modes of the *Chitta* (mind-stuff), it continues to experience pleasure and pain through numerous embodiments, but when it ascends the heights of meditation and *Samadhi*, it begins to discover its mastery over *Prakriti* and its independence from it. However, until this discovery is complete, the contact between *Purusha* and *Prakriti* is maintained.

The cause of this contact is further explained in the following Sutra.

Sutra 24

तस्य हेतुरविद्या

TASYA HETURAVIDYA.

TASYA: Of contact. HETUH: The cause. AVIDYA: Ignorance.

Meaning

Ignorance is the cause of this contact.

Explanation

Sutra 5 of this chapter explains the nature of *Avidya*. The following Sutra speaks of *Hana* or the cessation of pain in the state of Liberation.

Sutra 25

तदभावात्संयोगाभावो हानं तद्दृशेः कैवल्यम्

TADABHAVAT SAMYOGABHAVO HANAM TADRISHEH KAIVALYAM.

TAD: That. ABHAVAT: By the removal. SAMYOGA: Contact. ABHAVO: The end of. HANAM: Cessation of pain. TAD: That. DRISHEH: Of thee Seer. KAIVALYAM: Liberation.

Meaning

With the removal of ignorance, there is the end of contact; this is known as the Liberation of the Seer.

Explanation

When ignorance is removed by knowledge (*Viveka Khyati*), the seer (*Purusha* or the Self) in man is no longer associated with the *Chitta* (mind-stuff), which is an effect of the seen (*Prakriti* or Nature). This is the goal of the Yogic movement and is known as *Kaivalya* (Supreme Independence or Liberation).

The method of removing ignorance is described in the following Sutra.

Sutra 26

विवेकख्यातिरविप्लवा हानोपायः

VIVEKA KHYATIR AVIPLAVA HANOPAYAH.

VIVEKA KHYATIH: Intuitive knowledge arising in *Sasmita Samadhi*. **AVIPLAVA:** Unobstructed. **HANOPAYAH:** The means for the cessation of pain.

Meaning

Unobstructed development of intuitive knowledge is the means for the cessation of pain.

Explanation

When the impressions of *Samadhi* completely replace the outgoing impressions of the mind, intuitive knowledge becomes unobstructed.
(RAJA YOGA: III, 10)

Sutra 27

तस्य सप्तधा प्रान्तभूमिः प्रज्ञा

TASYA SAPTADHA PRANTABHUMIH PRAJNA.

TASYA: His (of the person who has attained intuitional knowledge). SAPTADHA: Seven types. PRANTABHUMIH: At the final stage. PRAJNA: Wisdom.

Meaning

At the final stage, the wisdom of a Yogi who has practised unobstructed intuitive knowledge is of seven types.

Explanation

The Yogi who has attained the highest degree of Yoga possesses a mind free from *Avarana* (the veil of ignorance), *Vikshepa* (distractions caused by subtle desires), and *Mala* (impurities such as greed and jealousy).

His lofty experience can be described in the following seven ways. The first four refer to the subjective aspect of Liberation, while the last three refer to the objective.

1. *Jneyashunya Avastha*: "I have known all that was to be known." For a Liberated Yogi, the world of the "knowable" has shrunk to nothingness. It is *Prakriti* that expresses itself in the world of the knowable objects, but when the purpose of *Prakriti* is fulfilled, nothing remains to be known.

2. *Heyashunya Avastha*: *Heya* or pain that is to be abandoned no longer exists for a Yogi. The contact between the seer and seen, which was the cause of pain, has been destroyed by the removal of *Avidya* or ignorance.

3. *Prapyaprajta Avastha*: "I have attained all that was to be attained." During Yogic practice an aspirant endeavors to attain the state of Liberation through the ascending heights of *Samadhi*. But once the highest state of attainment is achieved, there is nothing more to be acquired.

4. *Chikirshashunya Avastha*: "I have done all that was to be done." With the dawning of intuitional knowledge, the Spirit becomes released from the fetters of Karmas (actions). Having performed the highest act in the form of maintaining an unobstructed flow of mind to the Self, a Yogi has nothing more to do.

The following three, the objective aspects of Liberation, describe the release of a Yogi from *Prakriti*.

5. *Chitta Kritarthata*: The *Chitta* of a Yogi has fulfilled its purpose. It has given both enjoyment (experience) to the soul (*Bhoga*) and release (*Apavarga*), and is no longer needed.

6. *Gunalinata*: The *Chitta* now returns to its source, *Prakriti*, consisting of the three *Gunas* or modes of Nature.

7. *Atmasthiti*: The *Purusha* or the seer is established in its essential nature. There is no longer any identification with the thought-waves of the *Chitta*, and there is no longer the whirling wheel of birth and death. The Yogi will not return to this world-process anymore.

When the *Prarabdha Karma* (fructifying Karma) of a liberated Yogi has not been exhausted, he is known as a *Jivanmukta* (Liberated in life). He continues to live and to act in this world with a placid vision of inner freedom, and he does not generate new Karmas. But when the *Prarabdha Karma* is exhausted, the *Chitta* returns to its source, and the Sage is called a *Videhamukta* — Liberated without the body.

The method of attaining *Viveka Khyati* or intuitive knowledge is described in the following Sutra.

Sutra 28

योगाङ्गानुष्ठानादशुद्धिक्षये ज्ञानदीप्तिरा विवेकख्यातेः

YOGANGA ANUSHTHANAT ASHUDDHIKSHAYE JNANDEEPTIRAVIVEKAKHYATEH.

YOGA ANGA: The (eight) limbs of Yoga. ANUSHTHANAT: By the practice of. ASHUDDHI: Impurity. KSHAYE: Having been destroyed. JNANDEEPTIR: The light of knowledge. AVIVEKA KHYATEH: Until the attainment of intuitive knowledge.

Meaning

By the practice of the (eight) limbs of Yoga, the impurities (of the *Chitta*) are destroyed; consequently the light of knowledge begins to grow until intuitive knowledge is attained.

Explanation

A Yogi practises the eight limbs of Yoga which will be described in the following Sutras. As a result of this practice, the impurities of the *Chitta*, as described in the previous Sutra, are destroyed. And as this destruction continues, the light of knowledge shines brighter and brighter until intuition is in full bloom.

The eight limbs of *Raja Yoga* are enumerated in the following Sutra.

Sutra 29

यमनियमासनप्राणायामप्रत्याहारधारणाध्यानसमाधयोऽष्टावङ्गानि

YAMA NIYAMA ASANA PRANAYAMA PRATYAHARA DHARANA DHYANA SAMADHAYO ASHTA ANGANI.

YAMA: Ethical restraints. NIYAMA: Ethical observances. ASANA: Physical poses. PRANAYAMA: Practice of breath control for absorbing *Pranic* energy. PRATYAHARA: Withdrawal of the senses. DHARANA: Concentration of the mind. DHYANA: Meditation. SAMADHAYO: Superconsciousness. ASHTA: Eight. ANGANI: Limbs.

Meaning

These are the eight limbs of Yoga: *Yama, Niyama, Asana, Pranayama, Pratyahara, Dharana, Dhyana*, and *Samadhi*.

THE EIGHT LIMBS OF RAJA YOGA

VAHIRANGA
(External)

1. YAMA
   (Restraints)
2. NIYAMA
   (Observances)
3. ASANA
   (Poses)
4. PRANAYAMA
   (Breathing exercises)
5. PRATYAHARA
   (Withdrawal of the senses)

ANTARANGA
(Internal)

6. DHARANA
   (Concentration)
7. DHYANA
   (Meditation)
8. SAMADHI
   (Superconsciousness)

Explanation

The first five limbs are called the external means and the last three are called the internal means of *Raja Yoga*. Each limb is explained in the following Sutras.

Sutra 30

अहिंसासत्यास्तेयब्रह्मचर्यापरिग्रहा यमाः

AHIMSA SATYA ASTEYA BRAHMACHARYA APARIGRAHA YAMAH.

AHIMSA: Non-violence. SATYA: Abstinence from falsehood. ASTEYA: Non-stealing. BRAHMACHARYA: Abstinence from sex-pleasure. APARIGRAHA: Non-covetousness. YAMAH: These are the restraints.

Meaning

These are the restraints (*Yamas*): Non-violence, Abstinence from falsehood (Truthfulness), Non-stealing, Abstinence from sex-pleasure (Sex-sublimation), and Non-covetousness.

Explanation

Ahimsa or non-violence is the mother of all virtues and is called the highest virtue (*Paramo Dharmah*). *Himsa* or violence is practised in three ways: physically (beating or killing living beings), vocally (hurting others by sharp words), and mentally (directing ill will towards others). An aspirant must abstain from all these forms of violence according to his capacity. This virtue is founded on the spiritual fact that all living beings are expressions of the same universal life — the same Self dwells in all, and Universal Love is synonymous with the practice of non-violence.

Refraining from falsehood and speaking the truth is implied in the practice of *Satya*. However, one must not speak the truth for the purpose of hurting others. There is a popular saying, "*Satyam Vada, Priyam Vada, Na Vada Satyam Apriyam.* — Speak the truth; speak that which is pleasant, but do not speak that truth which is unpleasant."

Asteya or non-stealing implies freedom from desiring, misappropriating or stealing the possessions of others.

Brahmacharya is the restraint over desire for sex-pleasure as well as indulgence in sex. The practice is intended to sublimate sex-energy into mental energy, thereby increasing the clarity of intellect.

Aparigraha or non-covetousness is practised by simple living and by possessing little. Instead of hoarding objects, one should live a life of utter simplicity, and the fewer the possessions, the easier it is for the mind to enjoy an atmosphere of peace.

Sutra 31

जातिदेशकालसमयानवच्छिन्नाः सार्वभौमा महाव्रतम्

JATI DESH KALA SAMAYA ANAVACHHINNAH SARVABHAUMA MAHA VRATAM.

JATI: Class. DESH: Place. KALA: Time. SAMAYA: Circumstances. ANAVACHHINNAH: Unobstructed or not limited by. SARVABHAUMA: Universal. MAHA: Great. VRATAM: Vows.

Meaning

These *Yamas* or restraints become great universal vows when they are not limited by class, place, time or circumstance.

Explanation

A person may not hurt people of his own class, but he may hurt others. He may not hurt a person in a temple, but do so outside. He may refrain from hurting someone on a sacred day, but do so on other days. He may not hurt others because of certain circumstances, but in other circumstances he may do so. As long as limitations are placed on the practice of these restraints, they are called little vows. But when these limitations are removed and when the restraints are practised everywhere, at all times, and without any form of hidden falsehood, they are called great universal vows.

Sutra 32

शौचसंतोषतपःस्वाध्यायेश्वरप्रणिधानानि नियमाः

SHAUCH SANTOSH TAPAH SWADHYAYA ISHWAR-PRANIDHANANI NIYAMAH.

SHAUCH: Purity. SANTOSH: Contentment. TAPAH: Austerity. SWADHYAYA: Study of scriptures (and repetition of *Mantra*). ISHWAR-PRANIDHANANI: Surrender to God. NIYAMAH: Ethical observances.

Meaning

These are the ethical observances (*Niyamas*): Purity, Contentment, Austerity, Study of scriptures (and repetition of *Mantra*), and Surrender to God.

Explanation

Shauch or purity refers both to physical and mental purity. Keeping the body pure and healthy by cleanliness and a pure diet is the practice of external *Shauch*, while keeping the mind free from jealousy, hatred, anger, lust, and other negative qualities is the practice of internal *Shauch*.

Santosh or contentment is keeping the mind free from desires for the objects of the world and remaining unagitated in all situations. A man of contentment is not affected by varying conditions in life, and, therefore, performs all his duties well.

Tapah or austerity consists in developing physical and mental endurance in different circumstances presented by daily life.

Swadhyaya refers both to the study of scriptures and to the repetition of *Mantra* (*Japa*). It purifies the mind and elevates one's thoughts to God.

Ishwar-pranidhana or surrender to God consists in developing the attitude that "I am an instrument in Divine Hands. Every situation and condition is ordained by God for spiritual upliftment." A devotee brings about supreme surrender to God by integrating his entire personality on the basis of increasing divine love, and he enjoys the spiritual sweetness that leads him to *Samadhi*, which removes all obstacles from his path.

The last three *Niyamas* — *Tapah*, *Swadhyaya* and *Ishwar-pranidhana* together are called *Kriya Yoga* — the Yoga that purifies the heart. This has already been briefly described in Sutra 1 of this chapter.

Sutra 33

वितर्केबाधने प्रतिपक्षभावनम्

VITARKA VADHANE PRATIPAKSHA BHAVANAM.

VITARKA: Wrong mentation. **VADHANE:** Obstruct. **PRATIPAKSHA:** Adapting the mind to a contrary process. **BHAVANAM:** Feeling or thought.

Meaning

When wrong mentations obstruct (the practice of the *Yamas* and *Niyamas*), one should adapt the mind to the contrary process of thought.

Explanation

Whenever the mind begins to entertain thoughts of anger, hatred, violence, passion, greed, or any other negative sentiment that opposes the practice of divine qualities, one should adopt *Pratipaksha Bhavana* in order to remove them. This is practised in three stages: 1. Detach from the negative thought (for example, the thought of violence), 2. Substitute a positive thought (for example, the thought of love and compassion), and 3. Bring about sublimation of the negative thought (as, for example, the thought of violence is converted into thoughts of love and understanding).

The nature of *Vitarkas* (wrong mentations) and the manner of overcoming them is further elaborated in the following Sutra.

Sutra 34

वितर्का हिंसादयः कृतकारितानुमोदिता लोभक्रोधमोहपूर्वका
मृदुमध्याधिमात्रा दुःखाज्ञानानन्तफला इति प्रतिपक्षभावनम्

VITARKA HIMSADAYAH KRITA KARITA ANUMODITA LOBHA KRODHA MOHA PURVAKA MRIDU MADHYA ADHIMATRA DUHKHA AJNANA ANANTA PHALA ITI PRATIPAKSHA BHAVANAM.

VITARKA: Wrong mentation. HIMSADAYAH: Violence, etc. KRITA: Directly performed. KARITA: Caused to be performed. ANUMODITA: Permitted. LOBHA: Greed. KRODHA: Anger. MOHA: Infatuation or delusion. PURVAKA: Joined with. MRIDU: Mild. MADHYA: Moderate. ADHIMATRA: Intense. DUHKHA: Pain. AJNANA: Ignorance. ANANTA: Endless. PHALA: Fruits. ITI: Thus. PRATIPAKSHA: A contrary process. BHAVANAM: Of thought.

Meaning

Violence and others constitute the *Vitarkas* or wrong mentations. They are either directly performed, or are caused to be performed (by others), or are merely permitted and encouraged. These *Vitarkas* are further joined with either anger, greed or delusion, and are either dull, moderate or intense. They give rise to endless pain and ignorance. Thus reflecting, an aspirant should take recourse to *Pratipaksha Bhavana* or to adapting the mind to a contrary positive thought.

Explanation

Negative mentations can be expressed in various ways. Violence, for example, can be committed directly by a person, or the person can appoint another to carry out the vicious act. Or one may simply approve of others who are indulging in violence. But in whatever form the act takes, it is all violence.

Further, one may be led to violence either by anger, greed or mental delusion. Further again, one may hurt others only in words or in some slight manner, in which case the act is dull. Or he may hurt others more effectively, and be active or moderate in his violence. Finally, he may go to extremes in which case his violence is intense.

An aspirant must be able to understand that every negative thought is to be controlled the moment it emerges from the unconscious. If a spark, which could have been easily crushed between one's fingers, is allowed to grow, a conflagration can result consuming forests. In the same way, any evil thought-wave must be nipped at the very bud. This is easy to do through the art of *Pratipaksha Bhavana* as explained in the previous Sutra.

Thus, an aspirant must control and sublimate every thought-wave that promotes violence, falsehood, impurity, greed, discontent, and lack of devotion to God. By doing so, he becomes established in the first two rungs of the ladder of Yoga, the *Yamas* and *Niyamas*.

Every *Yama* and every *Niyama* when perfected gives rise to a special mental power in the practitioner. This is explained in the following Sutras.

Sutra 35

अहिंसाप्रतिष्ठायां तत्सन्निधौ वैरत्यागः

AHIMSA PRATISHTHAYAM TATSANNIDHAU VAIR TYAGAH.

AHIMSA: Non-violence. PRATISHTHAYAM: When perfected. TAT: In his. SANNIDHAU: Proximity or presence. VAIR: Animosity. TYAGAH: Abandonment.

Meaning

When Non-violence is perfected, a Yogi acquires the power of subduing animosity in his proximity.

Explanation

When the mind is filled with universal love, it becomes very powerful. The higher mind of a Yogi dominates the lesser minds of vicious persons in a very short time, and if a person filled with anger and hatred finds himself in the presence of a Sage established in non-violence, he will be awed and bewildered. Furthermore, not only crude human beings, but also wild animals come under the influence of Yogis whose minds are filled with such a spirit of universal love.

An aspirant must profoundly understand the two aspects of the practice of non-violence: 1. Realization of the fact that one universal life flows in all, and 2. Therefore, one is not to live to hurt anyone in thought, word or action.

Lord *Krishna* says in the *Bhagavad Gita*, "He who is without hatred towards all beings, who is friendly and compassionate as well, who is free from the sense of 'mine-ness' (attachment) and egoism, and is equally balanced in pleasure and pain (such a devotee is dear to me)." *(XII, 13)*

Sutra 36

सत्यप्रतिष्ठायां क्रियाफलाश्रयत्वम्

SATYA PRATISHTHAYAM KRIYA PHALA ASHRAYATTWAM.

SATYA: Truthfulness. PRATISHTHAYAM: Being established. KRIYA: Action. PHALA: Fruit. ASHRAYATTWAM: Rests.

Meaning

By being established in Truthfulness, a Yogi acquires the power of achieving the fruit of whatever action he performs.

Explanation

Actions of those people who are not devoted to truth do not give expected results. On the other hand, men who pursue truth attain the power of invincible will, and their actions are never rendered fruitless.

Through the practice of truth the personality of a Yogi becomes so integrated that he is in complete harmony with the Cosmic Will. Therefore, his will becomes invincible — whatever he wills comes to pass; whatever action he performs, he attains success; whatever he says, comes to be true. His blessings become infallible.

Sutra 37

अस्तेयप्रतिष्ठायां सर्वरत्नोपस्थानम्

ASTEYA PRATISHTHAYAM SARVA RATNO-PASTHANAM.

ASTEYA: Non-stealing. PRATISHTHAYAM: When established. SARVA: All. RATNA: Pearls or wealth. UPASTHANAM: Attracts to himself.

Meaning

When a Yogi is established in Non-stealing, he acquires the power of attracting all wealth to himself.

Explanation

The term "stealing" must be understood in a broad sense. Guided by greed and selfishness, people rob others of their opportunities and misappropriate possessions which really belong to others. This vice is called stealing and is based upon the mental complex of greed and uncontrolled senses.

Even normal forms of wealth and prosperity cannot be acquired through a mind too limited by greed and selfishness. A healthy form of prosperity demands a certain degree of mastery over the mind and strength of will.

If the mind is freed from the humiliating complex of greed for more and more physical possessions, it will be able to draw to itself all types of riches, both material and spiritual. Nature flows in a greater abundance to the highly elevated personality of a Yogi, and he becomes an abode of all forms of wealth.

Sutra 38

ब्रह्मचर्यप्रतिष्ठायां वीर्यलाभः

BRAHMACHARYA PRATISHTHAYAM VEERYA LABHAH.

BRAHMACHARYA: Control of sex-energy. **PRATISHTHAYAM:** When established. **VEERYA:** Abundance of energy. **LABHAH:** One acquires.

Meaning

By being established in *Brahmacharya* (control over the sex-energy), one acquires abundant energy.

Explanation

The term *Brahmacharya* in a broad sense means movement in *Brahman* (the Absolute); but in a limited sense it is the virtue of controlling and sublimating the sex-urge.

When the vision of mental advancement and the joy of spiritual creativity emerge from deep within the heart, it becomes necessary for the aspirant to restrain the mind and senses from pursuing dissipating pleasures. Sex is a powerful factor in human personality. It is the creative force operating in the physical-vital plane of one's being. Its energy, which has the power of creating human beings, neither should be wasted under the dictates of passing sentiments, nor should it be misused. Rather, when it is properly channelized and sublimated, it gives rise to the development of a very high standard of health of the body and mind.

The sublimated sex-energy is called *Ojas Shakti* (effulgent energy) and is the basis of mental movement towards spiritual expansion during deep meditation. It is the basis for creative thoughts and ideas which have been the fountain source of all great works of sages, saints and men of genius in every field.

Sutra 39

अपरिग्रहस्थैर्ये जन्मकथन्तासंबोधः

APARIGRAHA STHAIRYE JANMA KATHANTA SAMBODHAH.

APARIGRAHA: Non-covetousness. **STHAIRYE:** Being perfected. **JANMA KATHANTA:** The knowledge of past births. **SAMBODHAH:** He acquires.

Meaning

By attaining perfection in Non-covetousness, one acquires the knowledge of past births.

Explanation

Parigraha or covetousness is the vice of hoarding wealth or possessions on the basis of greed. *Aparigraha* or non-covetousness is the virtue that stops one from a blind chase after increasing possessions.

Covetousness forces one to become involved in the realities of the present life alone. It obscures the knowledge that the soul has passed through many embodiments. When a Yogi perfects the practice of non-covetousness, he becomes detached even from his body, mind and senses. His mind then reveals the fact that the soul is never confined to the present embodiment alone; rather, it has passed through many embodiments. Further, he comes to understand that when he brings about the cessation of all cravings and greed, his soul will attain *Moksha* or Liberation. He will not be born any more.

The following Sutras describe the powers that arise by perfecting the *Niyamas* or observances.

Sutra 40

शौचात्स्वाङ्गजुगुप्सा परैरसंसर्गः

SHAUCHAT SWANGA JUGUPSA PARAIR ASAMSARGAH.

SHAUCHAT: By (the perfection of) external purity.
SWANGA: One's own body. JUGUPSA: Dispassion.
PARAIR: Towards other bodies as well.
ASAMSARGAH: Dispassion or disassociation.

Meaning

By the perfection of *Shaucha* (external purity), one develops dispassion towards one's own body and towards the bodies of others.

Explanation

Shaucha is of two types, physical and mental. This Sutra deals with the perfection of physical or external purity.

Maintaining a clean and healthy body by taking baths, observing proper forms of diet, practising healthy exercises, wearing clean clothes, and keeping external surroundings clean are all different forms of external *Shaucha*.

If the practice of external purity is maintained with persistence, an aspirant develops dispassion towards his body. He realizes that his body is merely an instrument and not the soul. Likewise, he develops dispassion towards the bodies of others. His relationship with others is not based on physical bodies and their appearances, but rather it is deep, profound and spiritual.

Sutra 41

सत्त्वशुद्धिसौमनस्यैकाग्र्येन्द्रियजयात्मदर्शनयोग्यत्वानि च

SATTWA SHUDDHI SAUMANASYA EKAGRYA INDRIYA JAYATWAM ATMA DARSHAN YOGYATWANI CHA.

SATTWA SHUDDHI: Purity of the heart. SAUMANASYA: Cheerfulness. EKAGRYA: One-pointedness. INDRIYA JAYATWAM: Control of the senses. ATMA DARSHAN: Self-realization. YOGYATWANI: Ability for. CHA: And.

Meaning

Mental purity gives rise to purity of heart, cheerfulness, one-pointedness (concentration of mind), control of the senses, and the ability to attain Self-realization.

Explanation

The practice of mental purity consists of keeping the mind free from hatred, anger, pride, jealousy, passion and all other shallow sentiments and desires that dissipate mental energy. Purity of mind is the key to all those excellent qualities mentioned in this Sutra.

Sutra 42

संतोषादनुत्तममुखलाभः

SANTOSHAT ANUTTAM SUKH LABHAH.

SANTOSHAT: By contentment. **ANUTTAM:** Unparalleled. **SUKH:** Bliss. **LABHAH:** Attains or enjoys.

Meaning

By being established in contentment, a Yogi enjoys unique and unparalleled bliss.

Explanation

According to *Yoga Vasistha*, there are four gatekeepers at the palace of Liberation: *Shama* (serenity), *Santosh* (contentment), *Satsanga* (good association) and *Vichara* (reflection and meditation). *Santosh* is closely associated with these other three great virtues.

Sage *Vyasa* states, "All the joys there are in the world based upon the fulfilment of desires and the pleasures of the astral heavens — all these put together are in no way equal to even a sixteenth part of the bliss that manifests when the cravings of the mind terminate on account of contentment."

Every form of pleasure can be excelled by another form of pleasure. But the bliss that arises on the basis of contentment is unexcellable. A Yogi of contentment does not depend upon outer circumstances for his happiness; he experiences the bliss of the Self through his purified mind.

Sutra 43

कायेन्द्रियसिद्धिरशुद्धिक्षयात्तपसः

KAYENDRIYA SIDDHIH ASHUDDHI KSHAYAT TAPASAH.

KAYA: Body. INDRIYA: Senses. SIDDHIH: Powers or perfections. ASHUDDHI: Impurity. KSHAYAT: Are destroyed. TAPASAH: By austerity.

Meaning

When austerity is perfected, impurities are destroyed and perfections arise in the body and senses.

Explanation

Austerity is practised in various ways. Enduring hot and cold, fasting, subjecting the body to various difficult conditions are forms of austerity practised on the physical plane. Observing silence and controlling the speech are vocal austerities. The practice of concentration, meditation and devotion, as well as keeping the mind balanced in pleasure and pain are mental forms of austerity. But austerity is austerity only if it is performed for the sake of mental advancement and spiritual unfoldment. Merely suffering through a painful condition without the proper attitude cannot be considered austerity.

Austerity purifies the body, mind and senses. Just as metal ores are purified by subjecting them to fire, so too the body, mind and senses are purified by the practice of austerity. Through austerity a Yogi acquires a healthy body which is immune to diseases and which is full of vitality, as well as a healthy mind. He develops the mystic power of supersensory perceptions in the form of smell, vision, taste, touch and hearing. Then, endowed with these powers, a Yogi proceeds further in order to realize the Self. *(RAJA YOGA: I, 35)*

Sutra 44

स्वाध्यायादिष्टदेवतासंप्रयोगः

SWADHYAYAT ISHTA DEVATA SAMPRAYOGAH.

SWADHYAYAT: By the practice of study of scriptures and repetition of Divine Name. ISHTA DEVATA: One's chosen Deity. SAMPRAYOGAH: Communion.

Meaning

By attaining perfection in *Swadhyaya* (study of scriptures and repetition of *Mantra*), one develops the ability to commune with one's chosen Deity (as well as with Sages and Saints).

Explanation

Swadhyaya refers to these three forms of spiritual practice: 1. Study of the scriptures such as the *Vedas*, the *Upanishads*, the *Gita*, the *Ramayana* and others, according to one's faith and understanding. 2. Repetition of *Mantra* with feeling and understanding. 3. Study of life.

In the absence of association with living advanced personalities, *Swadhyaya* provides the best means of *Satsanga* or good association. By such practice, one can place oneself in contact with Sages such as Patanjali, Valmiki, Vyasa and others, or great religious personalities such as Jesus, Buddha, and Moses.

By repeating the *Mantra* of Lord *Rama*, an aspirant develops the ability of having *Darshan* (the mystic vision and divine communion) of *Rama*. Similarly, by practising different *Mantras*, he can develop the ability of communing with the different Gods who are essentially different aspects of the Self.

From a broad point of view, an aspirant must feel that he is a life-long student in the university of the world. He must learn lessons from the book of life, and thus develop the art of cosmic love. By attaining perfection in this form of study, he entitles himself to commune with the Divine Self, the center and goal of life.

Sutra 45

समाधिसिद्धिरीश्वरप्रणिधानात्

SAMADHI SIDDHIR ISHWAR PRANIDHANAT.

SAMADHI: Superconsciousness. **SIDDHIR**: Success or accomplishment. **ISHWAR**: God. **PRANIDHANAT**: By surrendering.

Meaning

By surrendering to God (or when the practice of divine surrender becomes established) a Yogi develops success in attaining *Samadhi*.

Explanation

It has been explained in *Samadhi Pad* (Sutras 23 to 29) that *Samadhi* is attained by surrender to God, who is free of afflictions, Karmas, the fructification of Karmas, and the mind-stuff which is the receptacle of Karmas. By repeating Om and by meditating upon its meaning, one develops devotion to the Divine Self, a devotion which in turn blossoms into a complete surrender of one's personality. As a Yogi learns this mystic art of surrendering himself to God, he becomes increasingly free of mental distractions and various obstacles that proceed from them. Therefore, led by divine grace, his vision soars beyond the realms of the mind and senses.

The practice of the *Yamas* and *Niyamas* (restraints and observances) culminate in *Ishwar Pranidhana* which in turn leads the Yogi to the ascending heights of *Samadhi*, until the state of Liberation is attained. The following Sutra concerns the third limb of Yoga, *Asana* or physical pose, for the practice of meditation.

Sutra 46

स्थिरसुखमासनम्

STHIRA SUKHAM ASANAM.

STHIRA: Steady. SUKHAM: Comfortable. ASANAM: Pose (for meditation).

Meaning

A seated pose (for meditation) that is steady and comfortable is called *Asana*.

Explanation

To attain success in the practice of concentration, meditation and *Samadhi*, an aspirant begins by developing steadiness of a meditative pose.

Author Swami Jyotir Maya Nanda

As *Rajas* or the principle of desire and passion begins to diminish, a Yogi becomes physically more relaxed, allowing him to be able to maintain his body still, like a painted picture for a long duration. An aspirant trains himself to be seated in a cross-legged pose for three hours at a time, and, if he can do so without any discomfort, he has attained *Asana Jaya* (victory over the pose).

Hatha Yoga has evolved an elaborate system of *Asanas* (physical poses), *Pranayamas* (breathing exercises), *Kriyas* (purificatory exercises), *Mudras* (physical poses blended with mental concentration), and *Bandhas* (vigorous exercises for concentrating the *Pranic* forces in different parts of the body). By these exercises, a *Hatha Yogi* frees the body of *Rajas* and renders it a fit vessel for the practice of advanced forms of *Raja Yoga* in terms of concentration, meditation and *Samadhi*.

The art of rendering a meditative pose steady is given in the following Sutra.

Sutra 47

प्रयत्नशैथिल्यानन्तसमापत्तिभ्याम्

PRAYATNA SHAITHILYA ANANTA SAMAPATTIBHYAM.

PRAYATNA: Effort. SHAITHILYA: Relaxing. ANANTA: Infinity. SAMAPATTIBHYAM: By meditating upon.

Meaning

By letting go one's effort and by meditating upon infinity, a meditative pose is rendered steady.

Explanation

Led by thoughts of objects, the mind of a person continues to create tension in the nervous system. But when the mind is directed to the expansive horizons of the Self, it allows the body and its nervous system to remain in a relaxed state. Therefore, steadiness of the pose is easily perfected by a Yogi.

The mind must be directed to the boundless sky, or to the profound ocean, or to the form of one's chosen Deity. An aspirant does not try too hard to make the body steady, but rather, to relax his efforts. Once he has assumed a comfortable pose, keeping the spine, neck and head in a fairly straight line, the practitioner lets go all his efforts and allows his mind to imagine that it is, much like a swan, soaring in the vast blue sky. And the moment the mind becomes immersed in the joy of expansion, the body automatically and effortlessly becomes peaceful and steady.

Sutra 48

ततो द्वन्द्वानभिघातः

TATO DWANDWA ANABHIGHATAH.

TATO: By perfecting *Asana*. DWANDWA: Pairs of opposites. ANABHIGHATAH: Unaffected.

Meaning

By perfecting *Asana*, a Yogi is not affected by the pairs of opposites.

Explanation

Heat and cold, gain and loss, prosperity and adversity, praise and censure, pleasure and pain — these are the pairs of opposites that continue to keep human mind in a state of distraction. But the Yogi who has subdued *Rajas* (restless energy) operating through the body by the practice of *Asana* develops a balanced mind, thereby enabling him to endure the pairs of opposites.

Further, a Yogi who takes recourse to the various techniques of *Hatha Yoga* renders his body so strong and healthy that he is unaffected by the severities of weather. He can practise deep and profound meditation in heat or in cold, and he is neither pressured by diseases of the body nor by distractions created by the mind.

Sutra 49

तस्मिन् सति श्वासप्रश्वासयोर्गतिविच्छेद: प्राणायाम:

TASMIN SATI SHWAS PRASHWASYOH GATI-VICHHEDAH PRANAYAMAH.

TASMIN SATI: Having perfected *Asana*. **SHWAS:** Inhalation. **PRASHWASYOH:** Exhalation. **GATIVICHHEDAH:** Checking their movement. **PRANAYAMAH:** Is control of vital forces.

Meaning

Having perfected *Asana*, when the movements of inhalation and exhalation of breath are mastered, it is called *Pranayama*.

Explanation

Taking the external air in is called *Shwas* or inhalation, while expelling the air out is called *Prashwas* or exhalation. The breathing process in a human being is closely related to the subtle vital forces known as *Pranas*. In turn, the *Pranas* are related to the mind. Therefore, the Yogic scriptures emphasize the need of controlling the *Pranas* as well as the mind. When the mind is controlled, the *Pranas* are controlled; in turn, when the *Pranas* are controlled, the mind is controlled. And when both the *Pranas* and the mind are controlled, a Yogi ascends the ladder of meditation and *Samadhi*, and attains the highest goal.

Different types of *Pranayama* or breathing exercises are mentioned in the following Sutra.

Sutra 50

बाह्याभ्यन्तरस्तम्भवृत्तिर्देशकालसंख्याभिः परिदृष्टो दीर्घसूक्ष्मः

VAHYABHYANTAR STAMBHAVRITTIR DESHA KALA SAMKHYABHIH PARIDRISHTO DIRGHA SUKSHMAH.

VAHYA: External. ABHYANTAR: Internal. STAMBHAVRITTIH: Retention of breath. DESHA: Space. KALA: Time. SAMKHYABHIH: Number. PARIDRISHTO: Seen. DIRGHA: Long. SUKSHMAH: Subtle.

Meaning

These three types of *Pranayama* — internal, external and retention — are practised with relation to space, time and number, and sustained practice of

Pranayama leads to the subtlety of breath (and thereby subtlety of thoughts).

Explanation

In a typical form of *Pranayama*, a Yogi breathes in slowly through the left nostril while keeping the right nostril shut with the help of the thumb of the right hand. He keeps his mind relaxed and visualizes the inflow of cosmic energy into his body. This is called *Purak*. Then he closes both nostrils with the help of the thumb and the two little fingers, and keeps his mind focused between the eyebrows, visualizing the assimilation of cosmic *Prana* within his body. This is called *Kumbhak*. Then he releases the right nostril, and exhales very slowly and completely. This is called *Rechak*. These three phases of the *Pranayama* form half a cycle. A Yogi may practise twenty cycles or more of this type of *Pranayama* (alternate breathing) in one sitting.

While practising this typical *Pranayama*, a Yogi maintains a breathing ratio of 1:4:2. In other words, if he inhales for 6 counts, he retains for 24 counts and exhales for 12 counts. He must see that this process of maintaining the ratio is spontaneous. In the beginning he may not adopt the ratio, but rather he may practise inhalation and exhalation with a very short retention. As he adavnces, he will be able to follow this ratio for more effective results.

The term *"Dirgha"* in this Sutra refers to many variations resulting from the three phases of the above mentioned *Pranayama*. The variations are caused by adopting the three factors of time, space and number.

KUNDALINI YOGA

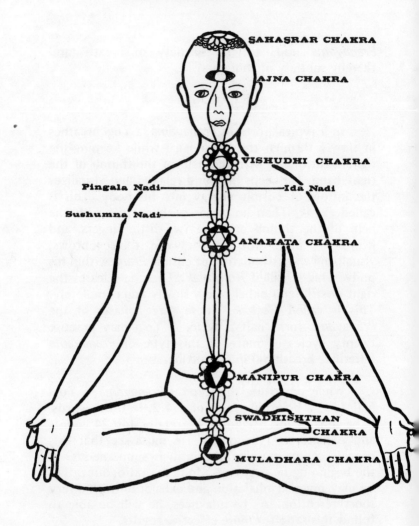

A Yogi arouses the mystic energy of the soul (Kundalini Shakti) by the practice of Yoga exercises and intense meditation on the various Chakras or centers; the awakened energy is led through the mystic channel in the spine (Sushumna Nadi) up to the crown of the head where the soul unites itself with the Absolute Self.

By time and number, a practitioner may measure his inhalation, retention, and exhalation of breath by mentally counting numbers, or with the help of a watch. By space, a Yogi measures the flow of *Prana* internally with reference to internal space within the body — for example, the movement of *Prana* from the *Muladhara Chakra* to the *Manipura Chakra* — or from the *Manipura Chakra* to the *Anahata Chakra*, etc.. Similarly, external consideration of space is adopted by measuring the flow of breath out of one's nostrils by placing a feather in front of the nostrils, and thus seeing the distance of the flow of breath.

As a result of these *Pranayamas*, the breath becomes subtle, leading to the subtlety of mind. A Yogi is able to make his thoughts subtle and sublime. *(RAJA YOGA: I, 34)*

Sutra 51

बाह्याभ्यन्तरविषयाक्षेपी चतुर्थः

VAHYABHYANTAR VISHAYAKSHEPI CHATURTHAH.

VAHYA: External. ABHYANTAR: Internal. VISHAYA: References. AKSHEPI: Renunciation. CHATURTHAH: The fourth *Pranayama*.

Meaning

The fourth *Pranayama* is that wherein the references of internal and external are renounced.

Explanation

As a Yogi advances in the practice of *Pranayama*, he rises beyond the considerations of time, space and number as described above. He is able to transcend his breathing process by the increased inflow of *Prana* within his system. However, it must be remembered that breath is not the *Prana*, but only an effect of *Prana*. Therefore, when an abundance of *Prana* flows within one's body, breath becomes increasingly diminished until there is a natural stoppage of breath. This form of *Pranayama* is possible only by advanced practitioners.

Sutra 52

ततः क्षीयते प्रकाशावरणम्

TATAH KSHEEYATE PRAKASHAVARANAM.

TATAH: By that (the practice of *Pranayama*). KSHEEYATE: Is destroyed. PRAKASHA: Light (of wisdom). AVARANAM: Veil.

Meaning

By that (the practice of *Pranayama*), the veil that hides the Light of wisdom is destroyed.

Explanation

Yoga Vasistha says that there are two seeds for the world-process: *Prana-Spandana* (vibrations of *Prana*), and *Chitta-Spandana* (vibrations of mind). When any of these two is removed, the other is also removed, thus leading to the destruction of ignorance and its effects.

The impressions of the *Kleshas* (the afflictions of ignorance, egosim, attachment, hatred, and clinging to life) along with their effects which are the Karmas that condition the soul, are refered to as the veil that hides the light of knowledge.

By the practice of *Pranayama*, a Yogi controls the vibrations of the *Prana*, which enable him to control the vibrations of the mind. This results in the attainment of the increasing light of wisdom until the veil is destroyed.

Wisdom continues to reveal itself as does the sun when clouds are gradually dispersed. When the clouds of mental impurities and illusions are gradually destroyed, the light of wisdom continues to shine brighter and brighter until it is fully revealed like the brightness of the midday sun.

Sutra 53

धारणासु च योग्यता मनसः

DHARANASU CHA YOGYATA MANASAH.

DHARANASU: In various concentration exercises. CHA: And. YOGYATA: Fitness. MANASAH: The mind.

Meaning

And also, the mind in an individual attains fitness for various concentration exercises (through the practice of *Pranayama*).

Explanation

It has been shown in the explanation of the previous Sutra that *Prana* and mind are interdependent. Therefore, as a Yogi attains success in the practice of *Pranayama*, his mind becomes increasingly composed and one-pointed. He can pursue various types of concentration exercises that are enjoined in the *Vibhuti Pad* (chapter 3) of *Raja Yoga*.

Mala (gross impurities of anger, hatred, violence, greed, passion, etc..) and *Vikshepa* (distraction caused by subtle desires) are the main obstacles to the attainment of success in concentration, meditation, and *Samadhi*. *Pranayama* promotes the destruction of these, and through its practice, a Yogi succeeds in ascending the rungs of Yoga.

The following Sutra explains the fourth limb of Yoga, *Pratyahara* or withdrawal of the senses.

Sutra 54

स्वविषयासंप्रयोगे चित्तस्वरूपानुकार इवेन्द्रियाणां प्रत्याहारः

SWAVISHAYA ASAMPRAYOGE CHITTA SWARUPA ANUKARAH IVA INDRIYANAM PRATYAHARAH.

SWAVISHAYA: Own respective objects. ASAMPRAYOGE: Being detached from. CHITTA SWARUPA ANUKARAH IVA: Follows the nature of the *Chitta*. INDRIYANAM: Of the senses. PRATYAHARAH: This is called *Pratyahara* or withdrawal of the senses.

Meaning

When the senses are detached from their respective objects and become as if of the nature of the *Chitta*, it is called *Pratyahara*.

Explanation

In *Raja Yoga*, the term *Indriya* refers to these eleven: the five senses of perception, the five organs of action, and the mind. These emerged out of *Ahamkara Tattwa* (ego-principle) which in turn evolved out of *Mahat* (Cosmic Mind), of which *Chitta* or the mind-stuff is the subjective counterpart in every individual. (Refer to diagram on page 84.)

As the *Pranas* are gradually controlled by a Yogi, he becomes aware of his increasing mastery over these eleven *Indriyas*. So much so, that even when placed in the midst of objects that are tempting to the senses, he is able to keep them withdrawn by his will.

The *Indriyas* follow the movement of the *Chitta*, just as bees follow the movement of the queen bee — wherever the queen bee goes, the other bees follow. So too, wherever the *Chitta* (or intellect) is directed, therein the *Indriyas* become involved. When the *Chitta* is withdrawn from the objects, the *Indriyas* also become withdrawn into the *Chitta* for the time being. When the *Chitta* becomes externalized, the *Indriyas* become outgoing.

For a Yogi who has attained *Pratyahara*, even a busy city becomes like a quiet cave. All words become sound vibrations, all sense-perceptions become mental fluctuations, and a Yogi experiences his mastery over them.

Sutra 55

ततः परमा वश्यतेन्द्रियाणाम्

TATAH PARAMA VASHYATENDRIYANAM.

TATAH: By that (the perfection of *Pratyahara*). **PARAMA:** Absolute. **VASHYATA:** Control. **INDRIYANAM:** Of the senses.

Meaning

By that (the perfection of *Pratyahara*), a Yogi attains absolute mastery over the *Indriyas*.

Explanation

Mastery over the senses is acquired gradually. When a Yogi practises restraint over the senses, he develops the virtue called *Dama* (self-control). When he begins to exercise his control over the mind, he gradually develops the quality called *Shama* (serenity of mind). When the *Pranas* are controlled by *Hatha Yoga*, the senses become temporarily detached from the objects, and is a gross form of *Pratyahara*. A higher form of *Pratyahara* is achieved when the mind is filled with dispassion. But all these are relative states of control over the senses.

When the Yogi becomes fully established in *Pratyahara*, he gradually advances in concentration, meditation, and *Samadhi*, and becomes detached even from the *Chitta* or mind-stuff itself. Then the *Indriyas* are withdrawn into the *Chitta*, and the *Chitta* in turn becomes diffused in *Prakriti*. This is the absolute mastery over the *Indriyas*. An enlightened Sage, though living in the world, transcends the *Chitta*, and thus possesses Supreme *Pratyahara*.

Thus ends the second chapter
known as Sadhana Pad
in the Raja Yoga of Patanjali Maharshi.

CHAPTER 3 — VIBHUTI PAD

Of the eight limbs of *Raja Yoga*, the first five, consisting of the *Yamas*, the *Niyamas*, *Asana*, *Pranayama*, and *Pratyahara*, are called the external means (*Vahiranga Sadhana*), and have been described in the previous chapter. The last three, *Dharana* (concentration), *Dhyana* (meditation), and *Samadhi* (superconsciousness), are referred to as the internal means to Yoga and are dealt with in the present chapter.

It is here by the practice of the internal means to Yoga (*Samyama*) that the immense powers of the mind are discovered and unfolded. However, an aspirant should not be led astray by the love of powers, but he must endeavor to go to the source of all powers, the Self within, for the attainment of Liberation.

Sutra 1

देशबन्धश्चित्तस्य धारणा

DESHA BANDHAH CHITTASYA DHARANA.

DESHA: Place. BANDHAH: To bind. CHITTASYA: Of the *Chitta*. DHARANA: Concentration.

Meaning

Concentration is binding the *Chitta* (mind-stuff) to a place or object.

Explanation

Concentration is the focusing of the mind on any point or object (internal or external), or on any idea. In ordinary cases, the mind is distracted; it has nothing to hold on to. But a Yogi who has acquired *Pratyahara* or withdrawal of the senses, focuses his mind on one point, object, place or idea for the practice of the deeper means of Yoga.

Sutra 2

तत्र प्रत्ययैकतानता ध्यानम्

TATRA PRATYAYA EKATANATA DHYANAM.

TATRA: In that. **PRATYAYA:** Of *Vritti* or thought-wave. **EKATANATA:** Continuity. **DHYANAM:** Meditation.

Meaning

In that (object of concentration), when the *Vritti* (thought-wave) of the mind flows on continuously, it is known as meditation.

Explanation

While concentration is the focusing of the mind at a point or at an object, meditation is the continuity of that focused state of mind. It is the deepening of concentration.

In the state of concentration, the mind gathers its rays or thought-waves from different objects of the world and focuses them on one object of concentration. In the state of meditation, the mind continues its focused state without interruption.

Sutra 3

तदेवार्थमात्रनिर्भासं स्वरूपशून्यमिव समाधिः

TADEVA ARTHAMATRA NIRBHASAM SWARUPA SHUNYAMIVA SAMADHI.

TADEVA: That itself. **ARTHAMATRA NIRBHASAM:** When the object alone shines. **SWARUPA SHUNYAMIVA:** The mind-stuff loses itself as it were. **SAMADHI:** Superconsciousness.

Meaning

That (meditation) itself becomes *Samadhi* (superconsciousness) when the object alone shines and the mind loses itself, as it were, in the object of meditation.

Explanation

When meditation deepens, one attains *Samadhi*. In the state of meditation one is conscious of these three forms of feeling: 1. This is the object meditated upon. 2. This is the process of meditation. 3. I am meditating. But when meditation deepens, the object meditated upon shines more and more. The mind becomes, as it were, lost in the object of meditation. One delves deep into the mysteries of the object alone without maintaining the feeling of "meditator" or "meditation."

It has been explained in the first chapter that the lower *Samadhis* are of six types: *Savitarka, Nirvitarka, Savichara, Nirvichara, Sananda* and *Sasmita*. *Asamprajnata Samadhi* is the higher *Samadhi*, and its perfection bestows *Viveka Khyati* or Knowledge of the Self.

The next Sutra describes the combined practice of these three: *Dharana*, *Dhyana* and *Samadhi*.

Sutra 4

त्रयमेकत्र संयमः

TRAYAM EKATRA SAMYAMAH.

TRAYAM: Of the three. **EKATRA:** Together. **SAMYAMAH:** The combined practice of concentration, meditation and *Samadhi*.

Meaning

These three (concentration, meditation and *Samadhi*) together are called *Samyama*.

Explanation

When concentration, meditation and *Samadhi* are practised together, it is called *Samyama*. Advanced Yogis practise *Samyama* on various objects which brings about the purification of the *Chitta*. Aspirants succeed in practising concentration and meditation together, but to acquire success in *Samadhi*, greater effort and more sustained practice is demanded.

When *Samadhi* is acquired, one practises these three together — in other words, one starts with concentration; concentration deepens and meditation begins; with the deepening of meditation, *Samadhi* supervenes. However, it should be noted that at this stage, the practitioner is not firmly established in *Samadhi*; after experiencing *Samadhi*, he may move back to meditation and then to concentration. But this practice, nevertheless, is called *Samyama*, because it involves the three practices together.

SAMYAMA

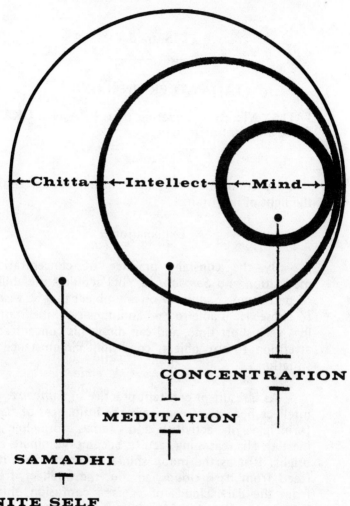

Concentration is the focusing of the mind on one object, idea or thought. Meditation is the continuous flow of one perception, and Samadhi is superconsciousness. These three together are called Samyama. A Yogi experiences increasing expansion of consciousness through Samyama, until he ultimately attains Self-realization.

Sutra 5

तज्जयात्प्रज्ञालोकः

TAJJAYAT PRAJNALOKAH.

TAJJAYAT: By conquering that. PRAJNALOKAH: There arises intuitive light.

Meaning

By conquering that (*Samyama*), a Yogi attains the light of intuition.

Explanation

By the constant practice of concentration, meditation and *Samadhi*, a Yogi acquires the ability of performing *Samyama* on any object that he wishes to chose. He is able to gain an intensity of meditation in a very short time, and can direct his concentrated attention to any object, condition, circumstance or situation.

As a result of constant practice of *Samyama*, his intellect becomes freed from the influences of *Rajas* (principle of activity) and *Tamas* (principle of inertia). His reasoning faculty becomes luminous and bright. Just as the moon shines effulgent when it is freed from dark clouds, so too, the intellect, freed from the dark clouds of egoistic confusion, shines bright with the light of intuition.

Though this intuitive light can be used for acquiring various psychic powers, which we will study in the following Sutras, its central purpose is to ascend the ladder of *Samadhi* in order to acquire Absolute Independence or *Kaivalya*.

Sutra 6

तस्य भूमिषु विनियोगः

TASYA BHUMISHU VINIYOGAH.

TASYA: Of *Samyama*. BHUMISHU: In the states or planes. VINIYOGAH: To be used.

Meaning

Samyama is to be used towards the different states (planes).

Explanation

A Yogi practises *Samyama* on the following planes:

1. Gross plane — In this plane he experiences *Savitarka* and *Nirvitarka Samadhis*.

2. Subtle plane — Here he experiences *Savichara* and *Nirvichara Samadhis*.

3. Subtler plane — At this stage the Yogi experiences *Sananda Samadhi*.

4. Subtlest plane — *Sasmita Samadhi* is experienced in this plane.

And finally, the Yogi transcends all these four planes of *Prakriti* through the practice of *Asamprajnata Samadhi*. *(RAJA YOGA: I, 45)*

Sutra 7

त्रयमन्तरङ्गं पूर्वेभ्यः

TRYAM ANTARANGAM PURVEBHYAH.

TRYAM: These three. **ANTARANGAM:** Internal. **PURVEBHYAH:** With reference to the preceding ones.

Meaning

These three (concentration, meditation and *Samadhi*) are internal with reference to the preceding ones (*Yama*, *Niyama*, *Asana*, *Pranayama*, and *Pratyahara*).

Sutra 8

तदपि बहिरङ्गं निर्बीजस्य

TADAPI BAHIRANGAM NIRBIJASYA.

TADAPI: Even that also. **BAHIRANGAM:** External. **NIRBIJASYA:** For the seedless *Samadhi* (*Asamprajnata Samadhi*).

Meaning

Even these (concentration, meditation and *Samadhi*) are external means for the attainment of seedless (*Asamprajnata*) *Samadhi*.

Explanation

With reference to lower *Samadhi*, the first five steps of *Raja Yoga* are the external means, while *Samyama* (the last three steps) is internal means. But with reference to the highest *Samadhi*, *Samyama* is the external means while *Para Vairagya* or supreme dispassion is the internal means.

The manner in which the *Chitta* (mind-stuff) undergoes its modifications during the attainment of *Samadhi* is described in the following Sutras.

Sutra 9

व्युत्थाननिरोधसंस्कारयोरभिभवप्रादुर्भावौ निरोधक्षण-
चित्तान्वयो निरोधपरिणामः

VYUTTHANA NIRODHA SAMSKARAYOH ABHIBHAVA PRADURBHAVAU NIRODHAKSHANA CHITTANVAYAH NIRODHA PARINAMAH.

VYUTTHANA: Outgoing. NIRODHA: Controlled. SAMSKARAYOH: Impressions. ABHIBHAVA: Suppression. PRADURBHAVAU: Emergence. NIRODHAKSHANA: The moment of control. CHITTANVAYAH: *Chitta* being involved in. NIRODHA PARINAMAH: Modifications of control.

Meaning

The suppression of the outgoing impressions (of lower *Samadhi*) and the emergence of the impressions of control (of higher *Samadhi*), such is the moment when the *Chitta* becomes involved in the modifications of control.

Explanation

During the practice of *Asamprajnata* (also referred to as *Nirodha*) *Samadhi*, a subtle modification takes place in the *Chitta* until it is resolved into *Prakriti*. This point is being clarified in this Sutra. As the practice of *Asamprajnata Samadhi* continues, the Yogi experiences the gradual decrease of the *Vyutthana Samskaras* (outgoing impressions) and the increase of *Nirodha Samskaras* (impressions of control).

Sutra 10

तस्य प्रशान्तवाहिता संस्कारात्

TASYA PRASHANTA VAHITA SAMSKARAT.

TASYA: Of the *Chitta*. PRASHANTA: Peaceful. VAHITA: Flow. SAMSKARAT: By the force of impressions.

Meaning

The *Chitta* attains the state of a peaceful flow by the force of the impressions of control.

Explanation

This Sutra explains the perfected stage of the process described above. When the *Nirodha Samskaras* have completely dominated over the *Vyutthana Samskaras*, the subtle changes of *Nirodha Parinama* continue uninterruptedly. This is known as the *Prashanta Vahita* (peaceful flow) of the *Chitta*.

Sutra 11

सर्वार्थतैकाग्रतयोः क्षयोदयौ चित्तस्य समाधिपरिणामः

S A R V A R T H A T A   E K A G R A T A Y O H KSHAYODAYAU CHITTASYA SAMADHI PARINAMAH.

SARVARTHATA: All-sidedness of the *Chitta*. E K A G R A T A Y O H :   O n e - p o i n t e d n e s s. KSHAYODAYAU: Disappearance and appearance. CHITTASYA: Of the mind. SAMADHI PARINAMAH: Modifications of *Samadhi*.

Meaning

'When the all-sidedness (distraction) of the *Chitta* disappears and the state of one-pointedness appears, the *Chitta* is said to undergo modifications of *Samadhi*.

Explanation

This Sutra along with the next explains in detail the process described in Sutras 9 and 10. Of the five states of the *Chitta* described in Sutra 4 of *Samadhi Pad*, the first three (*Mudha*, *Kshipta*, and *Vikshipta*) belong to most people who have not practised Yoga. Any change within their minds is called *Vyutthana Parinama* (outgoing modifications). But as one begins to practise *Samyama*, changes (*Samadhi Parinama* or modifications of *Samadhi*) begin to occur, thereby bringing about the replacement of impressions based upon the first three states of the *Chitta* (*Vyutthana Samskaras*) with the impressions of the fourth state of the *Chitta* (*Ekagrata Samskara*).

It should be noted here that Sutra 9 refers only to *Vyutthana Samskaras* and *Nirodha Samskaras*. In its context, when *Asamprajnata Samadhi* is practised, all *Samskaras* are considered as *Vyutthana* (outgoing) except the highest (*Nirodha* or those of pure control). But here in this Sutra, since the state of *Ekagrata* is considered, only the first three states are considered to be "outgoing" while *Ekagrata* is seen as "ingoing."

Sutra 12

ततः पुनःशान्तोदितौ तुल्यप्रत्ययौ चित्तस्यैकाग्रतापरिणामः

TATAH PUNAH SHANTA UDITAU TULYA PRATYAYAU CHITTASYA EKAGRATA PARINAMAH.

TATAH: Then. PUNAH: Again. SHANTA: Subsiding. UDITAU: Rising. TULYA: Similar. PRATYAYAU: Thought-waves. CHITTASYA: Of the mind. EKAGRATA PARINAMAH: Modifications of one-pointedness.

Meaning

Then, as the rising and subsiding of the thought-waves becomes similar, the *Chitta* undergoes *Ekagrata Parinama* (modification of one-pointedness).

Explanation

This is the end result of the process explained in Sutra 11. As the impressions of the first three states continue to be replaced by those of the fourth, a state is eventually reached in which the thought-waves of the *Chitta* flow from similar to similar, like the oil poured from one vessel to another, or like the form of a candle flame which appears the same but is always changing from similar to similar. Here the first three states of the mind have subsided altogether and the *Chitta* is said to have undergone *Ekagrata Parinama* or modification of one-pointedness.

The next change to occur in the *Chitta* is *Nirodha Parinama* (modification of control), as mentioned in Sutra 9, in which the *Ekagrata Samskaras* (impressions of one-pointedness) are

Author Swami Jyotir Maya Nanda

replaced by *Nirodha Samskaras* (impressions of control). The perfection of this state is *Prashanta Vahita* as explained in Sutra 10.

Sutra 13

एतेन भूतेन्द्रियेषु धर्मलक्षणावस्थापरिणामा व्याख्याताः

ETENA BHUTA INDRIYESHU DHARMA LAKSHANA AVASTHA PARINAMA VYAKHYATAH.

ETENA: By this. **BHUTA**: Elements. **INDRIYESHU**: In the senses. **DHARMA LAKSHANA AVASTHA PARINAMA**: Modifications with reference to *Dharma* (attribute), *Lakshana* (time) and *Avastha* (state). **VYAKHYATAH**: Have been explained.

Meaning

By this (what has been explained in the previous Sutra), the *Dharma*, *Lakshana* and *Avastha Parinamas* pertaining to the elements and the senses have been explained.

Explanation

Every manifestation has the following three types of modifications:

1. *Dharma Parinama* refers to modifications pertaining to *Dharmi* or the basic stuff. For example, a clod of earth is the *Dharmi* while a pot made out of it is its *Dharma Parinama* (modification of attribute).

2. *Lakshana Parinama* refers to modification in *Dharma* with relation to time. *Dharma Parinama* with relation to time is of three types —

(a) *Anagata Lakshana Parinama* — Subtle modifications in the basic stuff prior to the formation of the pot; at this state, the pot is in the future.

(b) *Vartamana Lakshana Parinama* — When the pot has come to exist and is in the present.

(c) *Atita Lakshana Parinama* — When the pot has ceased to exist or has been destroyed, and is, therefore in the past.

3. *Avastha Parinama* refers to modifications in the present condition. This applies to *Vartamana Lakshana Parinama*. A pot at the present continues to change from day to day, though the changes are not visible. This process of change continues until the pot disintegrates.

When applied to the *Chitta* and the *Samadhis*, the explanation is as follows —

Chitta is *Dharmi* (the basic stuff) which undergoes *Dharma Parinama* by giving rise to *Samskaras* (impressions); these *Dharmas* in turn undergo *Lakshana Parinama* (with relation to the three periods of time), of which the *Vartamana Lakshana Parinama* undergoes *Avastha Parinama*.

For example, for a Yogi who is experiencing the lower *Samadhis*, his *Chitta* (*Dharmi*) has undergone *Dharma Parinama* (impressions of one-pointedness) which is of three types: 1. Before the attainment of *Samadhi*, 2. During the attainment of *Samadhi*, and 3. After the lower *Samadhi*, i.e., when a Yogi enters into higher (*Nirodha* or *Asamprajnata*) *Samadhi*.

Again, the present state of *Samadhi* (*Vartamana Lakshana Parinama*) continues to change in intensity, giving rise to *Avastha Parinama*.

Sutra 14

शान्तोदिताव्यपदेश्यधर्मानुपाती धर्मी

SHANTA UDITA AVYAPADESHYA DHARMA ANUPATI DHARMI.

SHANTA: Past. UDITA: Present. AVYAPADESHYA: Future. DHARMA: Property. ANUPATI: Follows. DHARMI: The possessor of the property (the basic stuff).

Meaning

Dharmi (basic stuff) is implied as a basis for the past, present and future *Dharmas* (properties).

Explanation

Every object has infinite potentiality, and due to these potentials, each object will assume various forms. The *Dharmas* (properties or attributes) were in the state of indescribability (*Avyapadeshya*) before their appearance. These properties are hidden in the basic stuff and will arise in proper conditions. When a particular *Dharma* arises, it is called *Udita* (present). Having performed its function, it dies out and is then known as *Shanta* (past). *Dharmi* is implied as a basis for all these changes.

For example, water is *Dharmi* out of which different properties (ice or vapor) may arise, and the possibility of assuming one of these forms is hidden in it. When water is converted into ice, the basic water remains in its own nature. When the ice melts back into water, it still remains the same. In the same way, there are constant changes and variations in the external objects of the world, but the basic stuff out of which they are all fashioned remains the same; it underlies all modifications.

Sutra 15

क्रमान्यत्वं परिणामान्यत्वे हेतुः

KRAMA ANYATWAM PARINAMA ANYATWE HETUH.

KRAMA: Succession. ANYATWAM: Difference. PARINAMA: Modification. ANYATWE: Difference. HETUH: Cause.

Meaning

The difference in modification is due to the difference in the succession of changes.

Explanation

Different successions of changes give rise to different modifications. Water is frozen into ice. There is a succession of reducing the heat in the water that brings about the modification of ice. Even so, when heat is added to it successively, it is converted into water, and then into steam. This succession of change is true with all objects.

Having described the *Parinamas* (modifications) that have their sway over all objects of the world, and also over the mind and senses, *Raja Yoga* now proceeds to describe the *Siddhis* (powers) that are attained by practising *Samyama* on the three *Parinamas* described in Sutra 13 with reference to any object.

According to *Raja Yoga*, *Prakriti* is the basic stuff which modifies into all objects of the world. An aspirant is now instructed to recognize the *Dharmi* or *Prakriti* by intuitive vision born of *Samadhi*. The understanding of this topic is the key to acquire different psychic powers by the practice of *Samyama*.

Sutra 16

परिणामत्रयसंयमादतीतानागतज्ञानम्

PARINAMA TRAYA SAMYAMAT ATITA ANAGATA JNANAM.

PARINAMA: Modification. TRAYA: Three. SAMYAMAT: By performing *Samyama*. ATITA: Past. ANAGATA: Future. JNANAM: Knowledge.

Meaning

By practising *Samyama* on the three modifications, one attains the knowledge of past and future.

Explanation

When a Yogi performs *Samyama* on any object with reference to the three modifications mentioned in Sutra 13, he acquires the past, present and future knowledge of the object.

Sutra 17

शब्दार्थप्रत्ययानामितरेतराध्यासात्संकरस्तत्प्रविभागसंयमात्सर्वभूतरुतज्ञानम्

SHABDA ARTHA PRATYAYA ITARA ITARA
ADHYASAT SANKARAH TAT PRAVIBHAGA
SAMYAMAT SARVABHUTA RUTA JNANAM.

SHABDA: Word. ARTHA: Meaning. PRATYAYA:
Knowledge or idea. ITARA ITARA ADHYASAT:
Due to mutual identification. SANKARAH:
Confusion. TAT PRAVIBHAGA SAMYAMAT: By
performing *Samyama* on the distinctions of them.
SARVABHUTA: All beings. RUTA JNANAM: The
knowledge of sound.

Meaning

Due to the mutual identification of word,
meaning and idea, these are confused; but by
practising *Samyama* on the differences of these, one
attains knowledge of the sounds of all living beings.

Explanation

In our day to day experience, the mind of man
does not differentiate between word, meaning and
idea. These are mutually identified, as explained in
Sutra 17 of *Samadhi Pad*, and therefore, produce a
confused impression in the mind. But when the mind
of the Yogi is able to sublimate *Rajas* (the
externalizing force), he develops a keen intellect and
is able to differentiate between these three. This
endows him with a unique psychic ability which, if he
so desires, can be directed towards the understanding
of the sounds expressed by all living beings.

Sutra 18

संस्कारसाक्षात्करणात्पूर्वंजातिज्ञानम्

SAMSKAR SAKSHAT KARANAT PURVA JATI JNANAM.

SAMSKAR: Impressions. SAKSHAT KARANAT: By discovering. PURVA JATI: Previous births. JNANAM: Knowledge.

Meaning

By discovering the impressions, one attains the knowledge of previous births.

Explanation

By performing *Samyama* on the *Samskaras* (impressions) of the *Chitta* (see *Sadhana Pad*, Sutra 12), a Yogi can attain the knowledge of his previous lives. This power can also be directed towards other minds for acquiring the knowledge of their past lives.

Sutra 19

प्रत्ययस्य परचित्तज्ञानम्

PRATYAYASYA PARA CHITTA JNANAM.

PRATYAYASYA: Of the minds of others. PARA CHITTA: Other's minds. JNANAM: Knowledge.

Meaning

(By practising *Samyama*) on the minds of others, one attains the knowledge of their minds.

Explanation

Just as one can know his own mind by inward reflection, so one can know another's mind as well through concentration on his mind. For a Yogi who has attained the state of *Samyama*, it is easy to discern into the mental states of others. By meditating upon external signs, such as the color of the eyes, the appearance of a face and external movements, he can understand the nature of the mind of a particular person. He can know whether the mind is under the sway of jealousy, hatred, love or passion, or whether the mind is dull, agitated or partially concentrated. Such a *Siddhi* is of great importance for those working in psychology. By having such a power, they are able to help their patients by bringing to light their mental states.

The following Sutra is supplementary to this Sutra.

Sutra 20

न च तत्सालम्बनं तस्याविषयी भूतत्वात्

NA CHA TAT SALAMBANAM TASYA AVISHAYI BHUTATWAT.

NA: Not. CHA: But. TAT: That (*Chitta*). SALAMBANAM: With object (contents of the mind). TASYA: Of that. AVISHAYI: Not being the object of *Samyama*. BHUTATWAT: Being.

Meaning

But not the contents of another's mind, because, that is not the object of one's *Samyama*.

Explanation

By meditating upon another's mind, one realizes its state, but not its content. In other words, by the technique mentioned in the previous Sutra, one may know whether the mind of the person is agitated, calm, grief-stricken, etc., but one cannot know what has produced that state or what the mind's present condition is. This is all because, in the previous form of *Samyama*, the content was not the object of meditation. But, this Sutra states by implication that if a Yogi meditates upon the content of another's mind, he may, in fact, realize it. He may not only know the thoughts of others, but he may also know the cause that has produced those thoughts.

Sutra 21

कायरूपसंयमात्तद्ग्राह्यशक्तिस्तम्भे चक्षुः प्रकाशासंप्रयोगेऽन्तर्धानम्

KAYA RUPA SAMYAMAT TAT GRAHYA SHAKTI STAMBHE CHAKSHU PRAKASHA ASAMPRAYOGE ANTARDHANAM.

KAYA RUPA SAMYAMAT: By performing *Samyama* on the form of the body. TAT GRAHYA SHAKTI STAMBHE: The power of being perceived is checked. CHAKSHU: Eye. PRAKASHA: Light. ASAMPRAYOGE: Being separated. ANTARDHANAM: Yogi disappears.

Meaning

By performing *Samyama* on the form of the body, when its power of being perceived is checked, the light of the eyes is dissociated (from the form), and thereby the Yogi disappears.

Explanation

In every act of perception, whether of form, touch, smell, taste or hearing, the mind passes out through the respective sense organ and contacts the respective objects. Mind then envelops the object and brings it into contact with consciousness. Then the light of consciousness shines on the mode of the mind and illumines the object.

Therefore, in every perception these two factors are important: *Grahana Shakti* — the light of consciousness operating through a sense, and *Grahya Shakti* — the mind enveloping the object through a sense. When these two are separated, nothing can be cognized. A Yogi who practises *Samyama* on the form of the body, by the power of his will, separates the light of other's eyes from coming into contact with the form of his body. Therefore, although the Yogi may be very close, because of this *Siddhi*, he is invisible.

Adopting the same method, a Yogi may speak and not be heard; he may be near but may not be touched; he may have a fragrant flower in his hand, but the fragrance cannot be perceived by others. Ultimately he is able to separate the perceptibility of all objects from the perceiving consciousness of people by the force of his *Samyama*.

Sutra 22

सोपक्रमं निरुपक्रमं च कर्म तत्संयमादपरान्तज्ञानमरिष्टेभ्यो वा

SOPAKRAMAM NIRUPAKRAMAM CHA KARMA TAT SAMYAMAT APARANTA JNANAM VA ARISHTEBHYAH.

SOPAKRAMAM: Quick in fructification. NIRUPAKRAMAM: Slow in fructification. CHA: And. KARMA: Actions. TAT: That. SAMYAMAT: By performing *Samyama* on. APARANTA: Death. JNANAM: Knowledge. VA: Or. ARISHTEBHYAH: By portents.

Meaning

By performing *Samyama* on actions that are quick in fructification and actions that are slow in fructification, a Yogi determines the time of his death, or does so by studying the portents.

Explanation

Prarabdha Karma is the Karma responsible for one's present embodiment. It includes a portion of the *Sanchita Karma* (the storehouse of Karma from many past lives) and a portion of Karma acquired through actions of the present life. It is this *Prarabdha Karma* that determines the life duration of a person. Of the *Prarabdha Karma*, there are two types — the Karma that is quick in fructification and the Karma that is slow in fructification. A Yogi who performs *Samyama* on these two types of *Prarabdha Karma* is able to ascertain the exact time of his death.

However, there is a second method — people know the time of death by studying various portents, which are of three types: subjective, objective and divine.

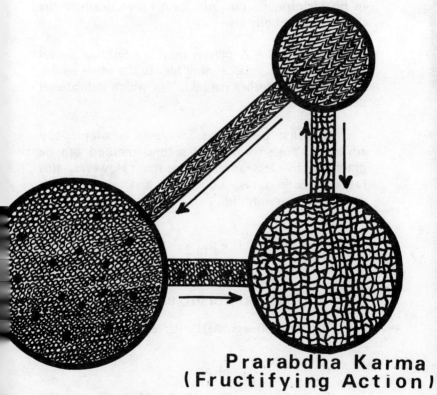

Kriyaman Karma
(Current Action)

Prarabdha Karma
(Fructifying Action)

anchita karma
ccumulated Action)

1. Subjective — When a person dreams of himself taking a journey on a donkey to the south, his death is near. Similarly, a sudden change in one's nature, such as a cruel man suddenly becoming compassionate, etc., shows the possibility of his death in the near future.

2. Objective — Certain external events reflect the future of a man. When vultures hover around his head, or when an inauspicious animal begins to howl in his vicinity, he can infer to his own death or the death of somebody else.

3. Divine — A person may see *Siddhas* (astral beings) in a vision beckoning him to the other world, or he may have other visions, all of which indicate his death.

The first method of *Samyama* is adopted by advanced Yogis, while the second method can be practised by less advanced people. However, this latter method is doubtful, and often such observations are invalid.

Sutra 23

मैत्र्यादिषु बलानि

MAITRI ADISHU BALANI.

MAITRI: Friendliness. ADISHU: Etcetera. BALANI: Strength.

Meaning

(By performing *Samyama*) on friendliness, etc., one acquires strength (corresponding to the virtue).

Explanation

By the practice of these virtues (i.e., friendliness, compassion, cheerfulness, and indifference — see *Samadhi Pad*, Sutra 33), an aspirant removes vices such as jealousy, hatred, malice, anger, etc., and acquires purity of the heart.

By performing *Samyama* on *Maitri* or friendliness, one develops the psychic power of befriending others; he develops a magnetic personality. Similarly, by practising *Samyama* on cheerfulness, he develops the ability of making others cheerful. The same applies with reference to all other virtues, for every virtue is capable of giving rise to a special type of spiritual strength.

Sutra 24

बलेषु हस्तिबलादीनि

BALESHU HASTI BALADINI.

BALESHU: Among strengths. **HASTI:** Elephant. **BALADINI:** Strengths, etc..

Meaning

(By performing *Samyama*) on various forms of strength (such as that of an elephant), one attains the corresponding strength of an elephant, etc..

Explanation

If a Yogi practises concentration, meditation and *Samadhi* on the strength of an elephant, he will acquire that strength. If he performs *Samyama* on the strength of a horse, he will have the strength of a horse. If he performs *Samyama* on the strength of the wind, he will acquire its strength.

Sutra 25

प्रवृत्यालोकन्यासात्सूक्ष्मव्यवहितविप्रकृष्टज्ञानम्

PRAVRITTI ALOKA NYASAT SUKSHMA VYAVAHITA VIPRAKRISTA JNANAM.

PRAVRITTI ALOKA: The light of *Jyotishmati Pravritti*. **NYASAT:** By directing. **SUKSHMA:** Subtle. **VYAVAHITA:** Hidden or veiled. **VIPRAKRISTA:** Distant. **JNANAM:** Knowledge.

Meaning

(During *Samyama*) by directing the light of *Jyotishmati Pravritti*, one acquires the knowledge of what is subtle, hidden or distant.

Explanation

During the practice of *Samyama*, as mentioned in *Samadhi Pad*, Sutras 36 and 37, and also in *Vibhuti Pad*, Sutra 5, a Yogi acquires a special intuitive vision, known as *Jyotishmati*, or the vision which is luminous. By directing this luminous vision according to his will, a Yogi can know objects that are subtle (atoms, subtle elements, *Ahamkara*, *Mahat Tattwa*, and all that is beyond the normal reach of the senses), hidden (such as treasure buried in the earth, pearls in the ocean, precious ores in mines, etc.) and distant (those objects that are situated in distant lands).

Sutra 26

भुवनज्ञानं सूर्ये संयमात्

BHUVAN JNANAM SURYE SAMYAMAT.

BHUVAN: World (universe). JNANAM: Knowledge.
SURYE SAMYAMAT: By practising *Samyama* on the Sun.

Meaning

By performing *Samyama* on the Sun, one acquires the knowledge of the universe.

Explanation

According to the *Puranas* (ancient scriptures supplementary to the *Vedas*), the universe consists of fourteen planes. This earth is known as *Bhuh Loka*. There are six above the *Bhuh Loka*, and seven below, totalling fourteen.

Samyama on the ''Sun'' is of two types — *Samyama* on the mystical Sun, referring to the light of consciousness, and *Samyama* on the physical sun. The former gives rise to the knowledge of the planes of existence while the latter gives insight into the knowledge of the physical universe or the earth plane, which includes the entire physical universe, and therefore, is of astronomical importance.

By performing *Samyama* on the light of the mystical Sun, one's consciousness rises above the body, and its all-embracing intuitive vision perceives all the worlds, their locations and descriptions.

Sutra 27

चन्द्रे ताराव्यूहज्ञानम्

CHANDRE TARAVYUHA JNANAM.

CHANDRE: Moon. TARAVYUHA: Galaxies of stars.
JNANAM: Knowledge.

Meaning

(By performing *Samyama*) on the Moon, one
acquires the knowledge of the galaxies of stars.

Explanation

Just as a Yogi acquires the knowledge of the
universe by meditating upon the sun, even so, he
acquires the knowledge of the galaxies of stars by
meditating upon the moon.

Sutra 28

ध्रुवे तद्गतिज्ञानम्

DHRUVE TAD GATI JNANAM.

DHRUVE: On the polestar. TAD: Their. GATI:
Movement. JNANAM: Knowledge.

Meaning

(By performing *Samyama*) on the polestar, one
acquires the knowledge of the movement of the stars.

Explanation

The polestar is relatively stationary, and
therefore, the movement of the other stars can be
determined with relation to it. By practising
Samyama on the polestar, the movement of the other
stars is determined.

Scientists studying astronomy naturally take recourse to a concentrated study of the movement of planets and stars. However, if they are endowed with the ability of *Samyama*, they can acquire remarkable success in their field.

Sutra 29

नाभिचक्रे कायव्यूहज्ञानम्

NABHI CHAKRE KAYAVYUHA JNANAM.

NABHI: Navel. CHAKRE: Center. KAYAVYUHA: Body. JNANAM: Knowledge.

Meaning

(By practising *Samyama*) on the navel center (solar plexus or *Manipura Chakra*), one acquires the knowledge of the body.

Explanation

The mystic center at the solar plexus is known as the *Manipura Chakra*. This center is predominated by the function of *Samana*, that aspect of *Prana* which performs the function of assimilation of food in the physical body.

By practising *Samyama* or intense meditation on this center, a Yogi comes to realize that the physical body is pervaded by the *Nadis* (subtle vital channels) through which the *Pranas* flow. Furthermore, through the practice of *Asana*, *Mudra*, *Kriya*, and *Pranayama*, he acquires *Nadi Shudhi* (purification of the *Nadis*) which enables him to gain insight into the vital secrets of the physical body. Consequently, a Yogi can possess a very healthy body.

191

Sutra 30

कण्ठकूपे क्षुत्पिपासानिवृत्तिः

KANTHA KUPE KSHUT PIPASA NIVRITTIH.

KANTHA: Throat. KUPE: In the pit. KSHUT: Hunger. PIPASA: Thirst. NIVRITTIH: Removal.

Meaning

(By performing *Samyama*) on the pit of the throat, (one acquires mastery over) hunger and thirst.

Explanation

The throat is the seat of *Udana Vayu* — the *Prana* that causes deglutition, takes one to dreams, and after death, takes one to the astral worlds. *Udana* is further responsible for the perception of hunger and thirst. Therefore, when *Udana* is controlled as a result of *Samyama*, there develops the ability of mastery over hunger and thirst at will. A Yogi can fast for a long time, and yet can maintain a higher level of vitality.

Sutra 31

कूर्मनाडयां स्थैर्यम्

KURMA NADYAM STHAIRYAM.

KURMA: Turtle shaped. NADYAM: In the vital channel. STHAIRYAM: Steadiness.

Meaning

(By practising *Samyama*) on *Kurma Nadi* (the vital channel resembling the form of a tortoise below the throat), one acquires steadiness (of the body).

Explanation

If one practises concentration and meditation on the *Kurma Nadi*, an astral channel that passes below the throat, one acquires steadiness of the body, because this vital channel exercises a benevolent and balancing influence over the entire body.

Sutra 32

मूर्धज्योतिषि सिद्धदर्शनम्

MURDHA JYOTISHI SIDDHA DARSHANAM.

MURDHA: Crown of the head. **JYOTISHI:** In the light. **SIDDHA:** Perfected being. **DARSHANAM:** Vision.

Meaning

(By performing *Samyama*) on the light at the crown of the head, one beholds the *Siddhas* (the perfected beings or the sages and gods).

Explanation

The awakening of every *Chakra* is characterized by the unfoldment of spiritual consciousness. When the *Sahasrara Chakra* at the crown of the head is awakened, it brings about the highest unfoldment of the spirit.

When a Yogi performs *Samyama* on the *Sahasrara Chakra*, he beholds the light of the higher Self. By continued *Samyama* on this light, he comes into contact with great sages and saints, the perfected Yogis and masters of spiritual Yoga.

प्रातिभाद्वा सर्वम्

PRATIBHAD VA SARVAM.

PRATIBHAD: By intuitional light. VA: Or.
SARVAM: All.

Meaning

Or all (this) is attained by intuitional light.

Explanation

Pratibha or *Tarakajnana* is intuitional light that leads one to the attainment of *Viveka Khyati* — discriminative knowledge of the Self or the knowledge that separates the Self from the not-self.

In the light of intuition, nothing is hidden or obscure. It penetrates *Prakriti* and all its evolutes. Whatever powers are acquired by special forms of *Samyama*, all of them are acquired by intuitional light without any effort.

Sutra 34

हृदये चित्तसंवित्

HRIDAYE CHITTA SAMVITAM.

HRIDAYE: In the heart. CHITTA: Mind-stuff.
SAMVITAM: Knowledge.

Meaning

(By performing *Samyama*) on the heart, one acquires the knowledge of the mind-stuff.

Explanation

The heart is the seat of the mind-stuff. The *Ajna Chakra* (space between the eyebrows) is the seat of the intellect. While exercising reason, a person concentrates at the *Ajna Chakra*, and he contracts the muscles between the eyebrows. But when a person experiences the unfoldment of feeling and deeper satisfaction in the heart, his face relaxes. This shows that mystically the heart-center is the support of the *Chitta* (mind-stuff).

Vasanas (subtle desires) arise from the *Chitta* and are mystically linked to the heart. Desires and thoughts arising out of *Vasanas* are linked to the *Ajna Chakra*, the region of the intellect. Meditation on the heart is the most effective method for acquiring the knowledge of the mind-stuff, and the purer the heart, the more one is able to meditate on the heart successfully.

This meditation leads to the knowledge of the *Purusha* or the Spirit, which is described in the following Sutra.

Sutra 35

सत्त्वपुरुषयोरत्यन्तासंकीर्णयो: प्रत्ययाविशेषो भोग:
पराथांत्स्वार्थसंयमात्पुरुषज्ञानम्

SATTWA PURUSHAYOH ATYANTA
SANKIRNAYOH PRATYAYA AVISHESHO
BHOGAH PARARTHAT SWARTHA SAMYAMAT
PURUSHA JNANAM.

SATTWA: *Chitta*. PURUSHAYOH: Spirit. ATYANTA SANKIRNAYOH: They are extremely different from each other. PRATYAYA AVISHESHO: The perception of identity of both. BHOGAH: Experience or enjoyment. PARARTHAT: Different from the perception of not-self. SWARTHA: Perception of the Self. SAMYAMAT: By practising *Samyama* upon. PURUSHA JNANAM: (One attains) the knowledge of the Spirit.

Meaning

The *Chitta* (mind-stuff) and the *Purusha* (Spirit) are totally different, but the perception of the identity of both constitutes enjoyment (or experience). By meditating upon the perception of the Self different from that of the not-self, one attains the knowledge of the Spirit (the Self).

Explanation

The *Purusha* or Spirit is non-active, non-enjoyer, and unattached. It is pure, immortal and indestructable. But due to the presence of the *Kleshas* (see *Sadhana Pad*, Sutra 3), the heart is rendered impure. For just as the moon is not reflected clearly in a lake having ruffled water, so too, the Spirit is not reflected clearly in a heart (the *Chitta*) affected by the impure impressions of the afflictions.

Due to ignorance, the *Chitta* and the Self are identified, though they are totally different. Just as clouds and the sky are totally different, even so, the mind-stuff and the Spirit are absolutely apart, and it is only due to ignorance that they appear to be identified.

The identity of the Self and the not-self (*Chitta* or mind-stuff) constitutes *Bhoga*, or the objective enjoyments (experiences) of the world (see footnote, *Sadhana Pad*, Sutra 13). This is the cause of bondage. But by meditating upon the perception of the Self devoid of the fleeting perception of the mind-stuff, by turning the vision from the fleeting to the eternal, one attains the knowledge of the Spirit. This leads to Liberation, and it is here that the role of *Bhoga* ceases. One then attains *Apavarga* or the state of Liberation.

Various other *Siddhis* that arise due to the practice of *Samyama* on the Self, and which are precursors to Self-realization, are described in the following Sutras.

Sutra 36

ततः प्रातिभश्रावणवेदनादर्शास्वादवार्ता जायन्ते

TATAH PRATIBHA SHRAVANA VEDANA ADARSHA ASWADA VARTA JAYANTE.

TATAH: By that (practising *Samyama* on the Self). PRATIBHA: Intuitive mind. SHRAVANA: Supersensory hearing. VEDANA: Supersensory touch. ADARSHA: Supersensory sight. ASWADA: Supersensory taste. VARTA: Supersensory smell. JAYANTE: Arise.

Meaning

By that (practising *Samyama* on the Self), one develops the intuitive mind through which the supersensory perceptions of sound, touch, sight, taste and smell are developed.

Explanation

By the attainment of intuitional knowledge, a Yogi develops all the supersensory perceptions. (RAJA YOGA: I, 35)

Sutra 37

ते समाधावुपसर्गा व्युत्थाने सिद्धयः

TE SAMADHAU UPASARGA VYUTTHANE SIDDHAYAH.

TE: They. SAMADHAU: For *Samadhi*. UPASARGA: Obstacles. VYUTTHANE: For the outgoing mind. SIDDHAYAH: These psychic powers.

Meaning

They (the supersensory perceptions described in Sutra 36) are obstacles to the practice of *Asamprajnata Samadhi* (the highest *Samadhi*), because these *Siddhis* belong to the outgoing mind (*Samprajnata Samadhi*).

Explanation

Attachment to any state of consciousness that is associated with matter is a cause of pain. These *Siddhis* do not allow a person to withdraw himself from the mind and its intuitive functions. Therefore, one desirous of attaining *Asamprajnata Samadhi* must develop *Vairagya* or dispassion towards them.

Sutra 38

बन्धकारणशैथिल्यात्प्रचारसंवेदनाच्च चित्तस्य परशरीरावेशः

BANDHA KARANA SHAITHALYAT PRACHARA SAMVEDANAT CHA CHITTASYA PARA SHARIRA PRAVESHAH.

BANDHA KARANA: The cause of bondage. SHAITHALYAT: By relaxing. PRACHARA: Movement. SAMVEDANAT: Knowledge of. CHA: And. CHITTASYA: Of the *Chitta*. PARA SHARIRA: Another's body. PRAVESHAH: Entry.

Meaning

By relaxing the cause of bondage and by knowing the process of movement, one's *Chitta* (astral body) is enabled to enter into another's body.

Explanation

There are three points involved in developing the psychic power of entering another's body, which are being explained as follows:

1. Relaxing the cause of bondage — The impressions of Karmas constitute bondage for the *Chitta* and remains as if tied to the body in order to reap the fruits of Karma. A Yogi is able to reduce these Karmic impressions, thereby allowing the *Chitta* to be free of and to transcend the body according to his will.

2. Knowing the process of movement — The Yogi then acquires the mystic knowledge of allowing the *Chitta* to move out of the body, travel in the astral plane and come back into the body. He gains an insight into the subtle vital channels, the *Nadis*, and

the *Chakras* of the *Sushumna* (the central mystic channel through which *Kundalini* ascends the *Chakras*), and the planes of existence that are associated with the *Chakras*. *(RAJA YOGA: I, 34)*

3. Entering into another's body — As a Yogi performs *Samyama* on the above two points, he becomes adept in entering other's bodies with the help of his *Chitta*.

The *Mahabharata* cites the example of *Sulabha*,* a lady endowed with this psychic power, who entered the body of King *Janaka* while he was seated on the throne, and held philosophical discussions with him. There are many other illustrations of Yogis who entered dead bodies in order to prolong their lives, thereby allowing themselves to complete the purpose of their existence. In other words, a Yogi who sees his own body becoming aged and incapable of spiritual assistance, looks for a dead body that is completely intact, enters into it and continues his Yogic *Sadhana*. By doing so, he allows himself to escape the loss of time involved in the process of reincarnation.

Sutra 39

उदानजयाञ्जलपङ्ककण्टकादिष्वसङ्ग उत्क्रान्तिश्च

UDANA JAYAT JALA PANKA KANTAKA ADISHU ASANGA UTKRANTISHCHA.

UDANA JAYAT: By conquering *Udana* through *Samyama*. JALA: Water. PANKA: Mud. KANTAKA: Thorn. ADISHU: Etcetera. ASANGA: Untouched. UTKRANTISHCHA: Upward movement as well.

*See THE WAY TO LIBERATION, Vol. II
by Swami Jyotir Maya Nanda

Meaning

By conquering *Udana* through the practice of *Samyama*, a Yogi is not affected by water, mud, thorns, etc., and he attains an upward movement after his death.

Explanation

Prana is the mystic energy that sustains life. According to its different functions, it is described in five aspects: *Prana*, *Apana*, *Samana*, *Vyana*, and *Udana*. *Udana* is the vital force that gives buoyancy to the body. It operates from the throat, its main center, and moves upward to the crown of the head. It plays a great part in dream, sleep and after death experiences.

By mastering *Udana* through intense *Samyama* on the *Vishuddhi Chakra*, the throat center, a Yogi sees his physical body as a projection of his astral body. He can then render his body so light and buoyant that he can walk on water, remain untouched by mud and pass through thorny thickets unharmed. After death, the Yogi follows the "Northern Path" of the enlightened souls. In other words, he secures the path of Liberation.

Sutra 40

समानजयाज्ज्वलनम्

SAMANA JAYAT JWALANAM.

SAMANA: The *Prana* that assimilates food. JAYAT: By attaining victory through *Samyama*. JWALANAM: Effulgence of the body.

Meaning

By conquering *Samana* through the practice of *Samyama*, a Yogi gains a "mystic effulgence" in his body.

Explanation

When a Yogi practises *Samyama* on *Samana*, (which has its seat at the navel center — see Sutra 29 of this chapter), he discovers the art of controlling it. When the *Samana* is controlled, all food taken by the Yogi is properly digested, thereby bestowing a high level of health to the Yogi; it is the key to the development of abundant vitality and spiritual magnetism, which is implied by the term "effulgence."

Sutra 41

श्रोत्राकाशयोः सम्बन्धसंयमाद्दिव्यं श्रोत्रम्

SHROTRA AKASHAYOH SAMBANDHA SAMYAMAT DIVYAM SHROTRAM.

SHROTRA: Ear. **AKASHAYOH:** Ether. **SAMBANDHA:** Relation. **SAMYAMAT:** By practising *Samyama*. **DIVYAM:** Supersensory. **SHROTRAM:** The ear-sense.

Meaning

By practising *Samyama* on the relation between the ear-sense and the ether element, one acquires the power of supersensory hearing.

Explanation

The senses are not the physical organs, such as the eyes, ears, etc. (in dream one perceives objects without the use of the physical senses). Rather, they are subtle processes of the mind. The ether element also is a subtle substance, and by practising *Samyama* on the relationship between the ether element and the subtle ear-sense, a Yogi develops the power of supersensory hearing.

Sutra 42

कायाकाशयोः सम्बन्धसंयमाल्लघुतूलसमापत्तेश्चाकाश**गमनम्**

KAYAKASHAYOH SAMBANDHA SAMYAMAT LAGHU TULA SAMAPATTEH CHA AKASHA GAMANAM.

KAYAKASHAYOH: Body and ether. SAMBANDHA SAMYAMAT: By meditating upon the relationship between the two. LAGHU TULA SAMAPATTEH: By identification with light objects such as cotton. CHA: And. AKASHA GAMANAM: The power of flying in the sky.

Meaning

By practising *Samyama* upon the relationship between body and ether, and by identifying with the lightness of cotton and the like, a Yogi acquires the power of flying in the sky.

Explanation

The element of ether is the basis for all the other elements: air, fire, water and earth. By practising *Samyama* upon the relationship between the body and the ether element, a Yogi discovers the art of reducing his physical body into the ether element, thereby projecting a body that is light and buoyant. Then the Yogi can fly in the air, or he can materialize and dematerialize the body, and he can transport his body to any place according to his will.

Sutra 43

बहिरकल्पिता वृत्तिर्महाविदेहा ततः प्रकाशावरणक्षयः

BAHIH AKALPITA VRITTIH MAHAVIDEHA TATEH PRAKASHA AVARANA KSHAYAH.

BAHIH AKALPITA: Mind existing outside the body, without imagination. VRITTIH: Perception. MAHAVIDEHA: Great bodiless state. TATEH: Thereby. PRAKASHA AVARANA: That which veils the light of wisdom. KSHAYAH: Is destroyed.

Meaning

The perception of mind existing outside the body, without any imagination, is called the great bodiless state, and this removes the veil of ignorance which obstructs the light of wisdom.

Explanation

In the beginning states of practice, a Yogi imagines himself outside of his body. He imagines that he can see his body just like a pebble by a river. When his meditation becomes intense, he perceives his mind to be independent of his body without exercising the power of imagination. Then he is said to have attained the state of the great bodiless awareness. This practice reduces identification with the body, and thus, enables a Yogi to develop intuitional vision of the Self.

Sutra 44

स्थूलस्वरूपसूक्ष्मान्वयार्थवत्त्वसंयमाद्भूतजयः

STHULA SWARUPA SUKSHMA ANVAYA ARTHAVATTWA SAMYAMAT BHUT JAYAH.

STHULA: Gross. SWARUPA: Basic nature. SUKSHMA: Subtle. ANVAYA: Qualities. ARTHAVATTWA: Purposefulness. SAMYAMAT: By practising *Samyama*. BHUT JAYAH: Mastery over the elements.

Meaning

By practising *Samyama* on the gross form, the basic nature, the subtle form, the qualities and the purposefulness of the elements, one acquires mastery over them.

Explanation

As the mind of a Yogi delves deep into an object through *Samyama*, it recognizes five planes of existence beginning with the grossest and ending with the subtlest:

1. Gross form. Every object has a name and a form dependent upon the perception of the senses. This gross form is only an appearance of a subtler reality, which is revealed as the meditation becomes more intense.

2. Basic nature. The basic constituents of all objects of the world are the five elements of earth, water, fire, air and ether. Each element gives rise to a manifest form, as water leads to the perception of liquidity, fire to heat, earth to solidity, air to movement and ether to spaciousness and expansion.

3. Subtle form. Further intensity of meditation reveals the subtle forms of the elements, which are mental radiations responsible for the perceptions of the senses. For example, earth element is characterized by smell, water by taste, fire governs sight, air sustains the perception of touch and ether is the basis of hearing.

4. Qualities. Deeper meditation reveals that the objects are dominated by the functions of the three *Gunas*, and that the five elements are in reality merely expressions of these *Gunas* of *Prakriti*. *Sattwa* projects the function of luminosity on the object, *Rajas* the function of activity, while *Tamas* projects the function of inertia on the object.

5. Purposefulness. Further, a Yogi discovers the spiritual purpose underlying the modifications of *Prakriti*, which continues to unravel itself through diverse modifications for the central purpose of enabling the individual soul to experience *Bhoga* (pleasure and pain) through life, and thus to advance on the path of spiritual evolution leading to *Apavarga* or Liberation.

Therefore, by practising *Samyama* on the gross objects of the world, a Yogi leads his mind towards the subtler planes of existence and discovers the Self as the underlying reality behind all names and forms. This enables him to acquire perfect mastery over all the elements. He then lives in the world as a master, not being affected by the world in any way.

The powers that are acquired and experienced by Yogis due to the mastery over the elements are described in the following Sutra.

Sutra 45

ततोऽणिमादिप्रादुर्भावः कायसंपत्तद्धर्मानभिघातश्च

TATO ANIMADI PRADURBHAVAH KAYA SAMPAT DHARMA ANABHIGHATAH.

TATO: By mastering the elements. ANIMADI: *Anima*, etc.. PRADURBHAVAH: Manifest. KAYA SAMPAT: Perfection (prosperity) of the body. DHARMA: Functions. ANABHIGHATAH: Not obstructed by.

Meaning

By mastering the elements, a Yogi acquires (*Siddhis* known as) *Anima*, etc., and develops perfection of the body, unobstructed by the functions (of the elements).

Explanation

Complete mastery over the elements places a Yogi in communion with the Divine Self. Therefore, he discovers the universal powers of God operating through his personality.

The eight major psychic powers are: 1. *Anima* — the power to become as minute as one wills, 2. *Laghima* — the power to become as light as cotton, 3. *Garima* — the power to become as heavy as a mountain, 4. *Prapti* — the power to reach any object, even if it were on the moon, 5. *Prakamya* — the power to fulfill any desire, 6. *Ishitwa* — the power to create objects and rule over them, 7. *Vashitwa* — the power to control the creation, and 8. *Kamavasayittwa* — Supreme Bliss arising out of complete mastery over *Maya* or cosmic illusion.

The following Sutra explains the perfection of the body.

Sutra 46

रूपलावण्यबलवज्रसंहननत्वानि कायसंपत्

RUPA LAVANYA BALA VAJRA SANHANANATWANI KAYA SAMPAT.

RUPA: Beauty. LAVANYA: Gracefulness. BALA: Strength. VAJRA SANHANANATWANI: Endurance like that of a thunderbolt. KAYA SAMPAT: Prosperity of the body.

Meaning

(A Yogi, as a result of his mastery over the five elements, acquires) a prosperous state of the body in the form of beauty, gracefulness, strength, and endurance like that of a thunderbolt.

Explanation

Perfection of the physical body expresses itself through beauty of form. The body of a Yogi develops a healthy symmetry, and due to the abundance of *Prana*, a unique luster envelops his body. This endows him with gracefulness and celestial charm. He becomes very strong, not only in his muscles, but also in his nervous system. His endurance during adverse conditions is as firm as a thunderbolt. He becomes immune to diseases, and he is unaffected by the ravages caused by the variations in weather and climate. *(RAJA YOGA: III, 40)*

Sutra 47

ग्रहणस्वरूपास्मितान्वयार्थवत्त्वसंयमादिन्द्रियजयः

GRAHANA SWARUPA ASMITA ANVAYA ARTHAVATTWA SAMYAMAT INDRIYA JAYAH.

GRAHANA: Instruments of perception (the senses). SWARUPA: The nature of the senses. ASMITA: Ego-center (the source of the senses). ANVAYA: The three *Gunas* (the underlying analysis of the senses). ARTHAVATTWA: Purposefulness. SAMYAMAT: By the practice of *Samyama*. INDRIYA JAYAH: Mastery over the senses.

Meaning

By practising *Samyama* on the senses, their nature, their source in the form of ego-center, their analysis in the form of the three *Gunas*, and their purposefulness in the form of enjoyment and release, a Yogi acquires mastery over them.

Explanation

This technique is similar to that of Sutra 44, except that instead of mastering the elements, here the Yogi masters the senses. Through *Samyama*, again he recognizes the five planes of existence, beginning with the grossest and ending with the subtlest.

1. *Grahana* or the gross form of the senses. This is the state of the 11 *Indriyas* (see footnote, *Samadhi Pad*, Sutra 15) while they are in contact with the objects. In other words, this is the grossest state of the *Indriyas*.

2. Basic nature. This refers to the *Indriyas* as they exist in themselves without objects; here they belong to the plane of the subtle elements.

3. *Asmita* or ego-principle (the subtle form). The 11 *Indriyas* arise from the ego-principle, the source of the *Indriyas*, which is the next plane to be recognized.

4. Qualities or analysis. The ego-principle is the product of the three *Gunas* of *Prakriti*. Therefore, *Sattwa*, *Rajas* and *Tamas*, the subtlest analysis of the *Indriyas*, are the next constituents to be recognized.

5. Purposefulness. Here the same meaning is unfolded as stated in Sutra 44, that is, *Bhoga* and *Apavarga* are the central purposes for which the senses operate.

The powers that are acquired by Yogis due to the mastery over these *Indriyas* are now described in the following Sutra.

Sutra 48

ततो मनोजवित्वं विकरणभावः प्रधानजयश्च

TATO MANO JAVITTWAM VIKARANA BHAVAH PRADHANA JAYAH CHA.

TATO: Thereby (by mastering the senses). MANO JAVITTWAM: Movement like the mind. VIKARANA BHAVAH: Perception without depending upon the body and senses. PRADHANA JAYAH: Mastery over *Prakriti* or Nature. CHA: And.

Meaning

Thereby (by mastering the senses), a Yogi acquires the power of moving with the speed of the mind. He perceives without depending upon the physical body and its organs, and he also attains complete mastery over *Prakriti* or Nature.

Explanation

In the process of mastering the senses, as a Yogi ascends the subtler planes of existence, he experiences the following *Siddhis*:

1. *Mano Javittwam*. A Yogi can move to any distant place as quickly as his mind thinks of it. In other words, a Yogi is more identified with his mind and senses than with the body. Endowed with mastery over the elements, he develops the psychic power of materializing and dematerializing his body at will, and therefore, he can appear at a distant place within a moment.

2. *Vikarana Bhavah*. His mind and senses develop the ability of contacting any object without the help of the physical body; they become absolutely independent of the body. *(RAJA YOGA: III, 43)*

3. *Pradhana Jayah*. When a Yogi attains the highest level of this technique, he is able to master the three *Gunas*, which constitute *Prakriti*. He can merge himself in *Prakriti*, the material cause of the world. This is also known as *Prakritilaya* (merger in *Prakriti*). *(RAJA YOGA: I, 19)*

Sutra 49

सत्त्वपुरुषान्यताख्यातिमात्रस्य सर्वभावाधिष्ठातृत्वं सर्वज्ञातृत्वं च

SATTWA PURUSHA ANYATHAKHYATI MATRASYA SARVA BHAVA ADHISHTHATRITWAM SARVAJNATRITWAM CHA.

SATTWA: Purified *Chitta*. PURUSHA: Spirit. ANYATHAKHYATI MATRASYA: Mere perception of the difference. SARVA BHAVA ADHISHTHATRITWAM: Mastery over all the Modes of Nature. SARVAJNATRITWAM: Omniscience. CHA: And.

Meaning

(By practising *Samyama* on) the difference between the *Chitta* and the Spirit, he acquires mastery over all the modifications of Nature, as well as the quality of omniscience.

Explanation

As a Yogi continues to delve deep into the mysteries of the elements, the senses and the mind, he comes to possess a highly purified *Chitta* which ultimately blooms into *Viveka Khyati* — intuitive knowledge that separates Spirit from matter. Then the Yogi sees himself as separate from *Prakriti*, and is thereby no longer dependent upon *Prakriti* and its modifications; he sees himself as omniscient — an absolute master of the entire creation.

A Yogi experiencing *Viveka Khyati* can, if he so desires, develop the power mentioned in this Sutra. However, the following Sutra emphasizes the need of removing this *Siddhi* for the attainment of Liberation.

Sutra 50

तद्वैराग्यादपि दोषबीजक्षये कैवल्यम्

TAD VAIRAGYADAPI DOSHA BIJA KSHAYE KAIVALYAM.

TAD VAIRAGYADAPI: By developing dispassion towards the aforesaid development. DOSHA BIJA KSHAYE: By the destruction of the root of evil. KAIVALYAM: Spiritual Freedom (Liberation or Independence).

Meaning

By developing dispassion even towards this (development of omniscience and supreme mastery over Nature), and with the destruction of the root of evil (in the form of ignorance), a Yogi acquires Liberation.

Explanation

As mentioned in the last Sutra, the Yogi's mastery over Nature and his acquisition of omniscience are the results of lower *Samadhi*. But as the Yogi advances beyond the lower *Samadhis* into *Asamprajnata Samadhi* (the highest *Samadhi*), he develops dispassion even towards these two *Siddhis*. He destroys the very seed or root of evil in the form of ignorance, and realizes the intrinsic freedom of the Self. With the veil of illusion lifted from his view, he sees himself as Absolute Existence, Knowledge and Bliss.* He becomes free from the cycles of birth and death, destroys the cause of pain, and experiences infinite bliss. Such is the nature of *Kaivalya* or Liberation.

*See VEDANTA IN BRIEF
  by Swami Jyotir Maya Nanda

Sutra 51

स्थान्युपनिमन्त्रणे सङ्गस्मयाकरणं पुनरनिष्टप्रसङ्गात्

STHANI UPANIMANTRANE SANGASMAYA AKARANAM PUNAR ANISHTA PRASANGAT.

STHANI UPANIMANTRANE: Being invited by gods of the celestial world. SANGASMAYA AKARANAM: One should not feel happy, nor should one be attached to their enjoyments. PUNAR ANISHTA PRASANGAT: Because there is again the possibility of an undesirable development.

Meaning

Being invited by the gods of the celestial world, a Yogi should not show happiness or become attached to their enjoyments, because there is again the possibility of an undesirable development.

Explanation

As the level of consciousness is elevated in a Yogi through the practice of *Samyama*, he begins to commune with the spiritual beings of higher levels of existence. The gods or the astral beings begin to covet the company of such a Yogi, and in turn, the Yogi develops the risk of being tempted by the subtle pleasures enjoyed by those beings. Therefore, Sage *Patanjali* warns an aspirant about being lured to such celestial company; he must continue to exercise his *Vairagya* (dispassion) at all times. It should also be stated that such associations may continue to be on a subtle plane, or they may manifest in the form of "visions" during meditation.

Sutra 52

क्षणतत्क्रमयोः संयमाद्विवेकजं ज्ञानम्

KSHANA TAT KRAMAYOH SAMYAMAT VIVEKAJAM JNANAM.

KSHANA: Moment. TAT KRAMAYOH: In its succession. SAMYAMAT: By practising *Samyama*. VIVEKAJAM: Born of discrimination. JNANAM: Wisdom.

Meaning

By practising *Samyama* on the moment and its succession, one acquires wisdom born of discrimination.

Explanation

Moment is the smallest conceivable division of time, and it is the succession of moment that expands into the ocean of time.

A Yogi does not allow his mind to be overcome by the illusion of time. Instead of directing his mind to the distant past and a remote future, he begins to focus his penetrating attention on the moment of the present.

Consequently, with his intellect rendered subtle by *Samadhi*, he is able to penetrate the illusion of time. For an intuitive mind, every moment is a gateway to eternity, and every object is a mirror reflecting the majesty of infinity.

Sutra 53

जातिलक्षणदेशैरन्यतानवच्छेदात्तुल्ययोस्ततः प्रतिपत्तिः

JATI LAKSHANA DESHAIH ANYATA ANAVACHHEDAT TULYAYOH TATAH PRATIPATTIH.

JATI: Class. LAKSHANA: Characteristics. DESHAIH: Place. ANYATA: Differentiation. ANAVACHHEDAT: Undetermined. TULYAYOH: Two similar objects. TATAH: Thereby (by discriminative knowledge). PRATIPATTIH: Determined.

Meaning

Thereby (by discriminative knowledge), a Yogi is able to determine the difference between two similar objects which are identical in their class, characteristics and place, and therefore, are difficult to be differentiated.

Explanation

Every object of the world is defined by class, characteristic, and place (occupied by it). A mind that lacks intuitive vision cannot break the illusion of similarity existing in similar objects, but when intuitive vision dawns, the mind is not deluded by the illusion of similarity, and thus, differences in objects are perceived.

Similarly, when the mind is unable to see differences between two similar thought-waves, it continues to experience a world of matter. But when it glimpses the underlying substratum from where the thought-waves arise, and into which they fall, it becomes intuitive. Likewise, the *Chitta* and the *Purusha* (mind and Spirit) have become identified due to ignorance, but by the possession of such discriminating wisdom or intuitive vision, the Spirit is seen as distinct from the mind.

Sutra 54

तारकं सर्वविषयं सर्वथाविषयमक्रमं चेति विवेकजं ज्ञानम्

TARAKAM SARVA VISHAYAM SARVATHA VISHAYAM AKRAMAM CHETI VIVEKAJAM JNANAM.

TARAKAM: That which takes one across the world-process. SARVA VISHAYAM: All-encompassing. SARVATHA VISHAYAM: Interpenetrating. AKRAMAM: Without succession (spontaneous). CHETI: And this. VIVEKAJAM JNANAM: Wisdom born of intuitive intellect.

Meaning

This wisdom born of intuitive intellect is all-encompassing, all-interpenetrating, without succession (spontaneous), and is that which takes one across the world-process.

Explanation

Intuitive knowledge includes all objects; once attained, nothing remains to be known. Further, such knowledge is a complete knowledge of all that exists — it interpenetrates the depths of all objects; there is nothing more to be observed or interpreted. It is spontaneous, having no intermediate agent such as the mind or senses.

Author Swami Jyotir Maya Nanda

Such knowledge takes one across the ocean of the world-process into the state of Liberation. It ends the process of birth and death, and enables the soul to experience the infinite bliss of its essential nature.

Sutra 55

सत्त्वपुरुषयोः शुद्धिसाम्ये कैवल्यम्

SATTWA PURUSHAYOH SHUDDHI SAMYE KAIVALYAM.

SATTWA: *Chitta*. PURUSHAYOH: Of the Self. SHUDDHI: Purity. SAMYE: Similarity. KAIVALYAM: Independence or Liberation.

Meaning

When a Yogi discovers the similarity of purity between the *Chitta* and the *Purusha*, he attains Liberation.

Explanation

This Sutra presents the goal of all psychic powers. A true Yogi discovers the powers of the mind with the sole purpose of attaining freedom from the clutches of matter. Discriminative wisdom or intuitive wisdom born of *Samadhi* is the highest power attained, by which he tears the veil of ignorance and realizes his essential nature as the *Purusha* (the Self).

In the previous two Sutras, it has been shown that the subtle intellect of a Yogi is able to tear the illusion of time and space. As a result of such penetrating insight, the *Chitta* (mind-stuff) of a Yogi becomes profoundly purified, and becomes free from the impressions of the *Kleshas* or the afflictions. The *Chitta* then reveals the *Purusha* without any distortion.

Chitta and *Purusha* both then shine with the same purity, as it were, and in this state, any confusion between the two is destroyed. The *Purusha* sees itself fully revealed in the *Chitta*, and thus, turns away from the latter. A Yogi has no need to use the mirror of mind to see his deeper Self. He develops dispassion even towards the *Chitta*, as well as towards *Prakriti* of which *Chitta* is the proximate evolute. Such a dispassion is termed *Para Vairagya* or supreme dispassion.

By the force of *Para Vairagya*, he then experiences *Nirodha Samadhi* or the cessation of all modifications of the *Chitta*. The fire of intuitive wisdom destroyes the forest of accumulated Karmas from the depths of his causal body, and he attains the goal of life, Liberation, which will be elaborated upon in the next and final chapter.

Thus ends the third chapter
known as Vibhuti Pad
in the Raja Yoga of Patanjali Maharshi.

*See YOGA SECRETS OF PSYCHIC POWERS
by Swami Jyotir Maya Nanda

CHAPTER 4 — KAIVALYA PAD

This is the concluding chapter of *Raja Yoga*, dealing with the ultimate goal of the eight limbs and the various disciplines associated with them. The ultimate goal is known as *Kaivalya* or supreme freedom from the world-process constituted of the three *Gunas*. The Spirit becomes free from the three *Gunas*, the five *Kleshas*, the Karmic involvements, and in brief, the endless cycles of birth and death occasioned by ignorance or *Avidya*. This same goal is known by various names: *Nirvana* (extinction of the flame of craving), *Mukti* (Liberation), *Nishreyas* (the highest salvation), *Parama Dhama* (the Supreme Abode), *Apavarga* (the Supreme Beatitude), etc..

It has been explained that the practice of *Samyama* (concentration, meditation and *Samadhi*) is the means of developing various types of *Siddhis* or psychic powers. Though this is true, Yogis endowed with the impressions of *Samyama* from their past lives may seem to acquire *Siddhis* by adopting apparently different means. This is explained in the first Sutra.

Sutra 1

जन्मौषधिमन्त्रतपःसमाधिजाः सिद्धयः

JANMA AUSHADHI MANTRA TAPAH SAMADHIJAH SIDHYAH.

JANMA: Birth. **AUSHADHI:** Medicinal herbs. **MANTRA:** Mystic formula. **TAPAH:** Austerity. **SAMADHIJAH:** Born of *Samadhi*. **SIDHYAH:** *Siddhis* or psychic powers.

Meaning

Psychic powers develop by taking recourse to birth, medicinal herbs, mystic formulas, austerity, or *Samadhi*.

Explanation

1. *Siddhis* or psychic powers arising out of birth. Due to the practice of Yoga in previous lives, a Yogi may be born with mystic powers. Many Sages were endowed with mystic powers even in their childhood, and were known as *Yoga Bhrishtas* — the Yogis who could not reach the highest state in their previous life due to some distraction or deviation from the path. But by passing through the process of birth, their obstructive Karma had been worn off, and therefore, they began to manifest various psychic powers from their very childhood. The divine incarnations such as *Rama* and *Krishna*, as well as various Sages and Saints such as Sage *Ashtavakra*, Sage *Vamadeva* (see *Aittareya Upanishad*), Saint *Jnaneshwar* and others expressed amazing psychic powers in their childhood.

2. *Siddhis* born of medicinal herbs. *Ayurveda* (the Indian science of medicine) has through many centuries made profound progress into the power of herbs over the mind and body. By taking recourse to certain herbal preparations, the body of a Yogi can be rendered invulnerable to various diseases and even to death, until he attains the highest state, fulfilling the purpose of his bodily existence. Various psychological impediments can be also removed by a blend of mental discipline joined with herbal treatment. It must be understood, however, that medicinal herbs by themselves cannot produce *Siddhis* in anyone, but wherever such is possible, it is

because they removed obstructions in the form of faulty functions of the body and mind, thereby allowing the past Yogic impressions to unfold into a state of perfection.

3. *Siddhis* born of *Mantras* or mystic formulas. Many Yogis, Sages and Saints attained various psychic powers by taking recourse to the repetition of *Mantras* alone, and specific *Mantras* can bestow specific powers. The *Mantra* of Goddess *Saraswati*, for example, endows one with proficiency in fine arts, the power of eloquence, literary and poetic abilities and in spiritual wisdom. *Lakshmi Mantra* endows one with prosperity. *Mahamrityunjaya Mantra* enables a person to develop healing powers. And *Mantras* of Lord *Vishnu*, *Shiva*, *Rama*, *Krishna* and others leads one to Liberation from the cycles of birth and death.

4. *Siddhis* born of *Tapas* or austerity. Austerities are of various types. They are designed to remove impurities of the body, mind and senses. Enduring adversity while performing one's duties is a dynamic form of austerity. Many Yogis and Sages from ancient times have attained great psychic powers by the practice of various austerities. From an advanced point of view, however, mental concentration and spiritual enquiry into the nature of the Self are included in the practice of austerity.

5. *Siddhis* born of *Samadhi*. The previous chapter has explained various *Siddhis* that arise by the practice of *Samyama*, and in fact, this is the ultimate road to the development of all psychic powers. Even those who take recourse to austerity, *Mantra*, or medicinal herbs, must enter into the heights of *Samadhi* in order to be endowed with the *Siddhis*.

The following Sutra explains what changes must occur in bringing about the development of psychic powers in the personality of a Yogi.

Sutra 2

जात्यन्तरपरिणामः प्रकृत्यापूरात्

JATYANTARPARINAMAH PRAKRITYAPURAT.

JATYANTARPARINAMAH: Transformation from one class to another. **PRAKRITYAPURAT:** Because of the flow of *Prakriti* or Nature.

Meaning

Because of the flow of Nature, there is a transformation from one class to another.

Explanation

In order to be endowed with psychic powers, certain changes or transformations must occur in the body, mind and senses. Such changes are possible because *Prakriti*, the material basis of creation, sustains and nourishes whatever is needed and demanded from her. Because of this, every human being is endowed with boundless possibilities, and when self-effort in a particular direction is sustained for a certain period of time, Nature begins to endow such a person with all that is needed for the desired attainment. A weak nervous system can be transformed into a strong nervous system, a weak mind into a strong mind, and various similar transformations occur as a Yogi advances on the path of spirituality. This is implied by the expression "flow of *Prakriti*."

Sutra 3

निमित्तमप्रयोजकं प्रकृतीनां वरणभेदस्तु ततः क्षेत्रिकवत्

NIMITTAM APRAYOJAKAM PRAKRITINAM VARANA BHEDASTU TATAH KSHETRIKAVAT.

NIMITTAM: Incidental causes. APRAYOJAKAM: Not mover (not urging *Prakriti* to action). PRAKRITINAM: *Prakriti* and its effects. VARANA: Obstacles. BHEDAH: Remover. TU: But. TATAH: By these. KSHETRIKAVAT: Like a farmer.

Meaning

These incidental causes (birth, medicinal herbs, etc.) do not urge *Prakriti* to action, but they merely remove obstacles, even like a farmer.

Explanation

A farmer, in irrigating his crops, allows water to flow from one level to the next, and from one field to another by simply opening or closing channels; his acts of opening and closing do not create the flow of water, but simply allow the water to flow by its own laws. Much in the same manner, when impure impressions (of *Adharma* or unrighteousness) are removed by pure impressions (of *Dharma* or righteousness), then *Prakriti* flows, endowing a Yogi with a subtle intellect, disciplined senses, a healthy body, and congenial circumstances.

As the obstacles are removed by the incidental causes such as birth, medicinal herbs, and others, the pure impressions of the past lives become operative, allowing *Prakriti* to flow in a favorable form resulting in various transformations in the body, senses and mind. Thus, a Yogi becomes endowed with various psychic powers or *Siddhis*.

Sutra 4

निर्माणचित्तान्यस्मितामात्रात्

NIRMANA CHITTANI ASMITA MATRAT.

NIRMANA CHITTANI: The transformed minds (as a result of the incidental causes). ASMITA: The source of ego-sense or *Ahamkara Tattwa*, which in turn links with the Cosmic Mind. MATRAT: Proceed from.

Meaning

The transformed minds proceed from *Asmita* (the source of ego) or the Cosmic Mind.

Explanation

This is a further elaboration of the previous Sutras. It has been stated that by adopting incidental causes a Yogi is able to effect certain transformations in his *Chitta*, thereby allowing him to advance on the path of Yoga. It has been further explained that through these incidental causes, a Yogi does not directly bring about such transformations in the *Chitta*; the true cause lies in the flow of *Prakriti*, which, like water flowing in various channels, flows into the personality of a Yogi as certain impediments are removed. The present Sutra states that these transformations actually proceed from *Prakriti*, of which *Mahat* (Cosmic Mind — the source of individual *Chitta*) is the first evolute.

Some commentators state that through his extraordinary psychic powers, a Yogi creates many bodies to exhaust his Karmas that obstruct the rise of knowledge, and the created minds in those bodies proceed from the Cosmic Mind. However, such an interpretation is irrelevant, because a Yogi can burn up all Karmas by *Viveka Khyati* without creating several bodies. However, all the powers of a Yogi are limitless.

Sutra 5

प्रवृत्तिभेदे प्रयोजकं चित्तमेकमनेकेषाम्

PRAVRITTI BHEDE PRAYOJAKAM CHITTAM EKAM ANEKESHAM.

PRAVRITTI BHEDE: In various functions. PRAYOJAKAM: The director or leader. CHITTAM: Mind-stuff. EKAM: One. ANEKESHAM: Among many (minds).

Meaning

The (pure) *Chitta* (of a Yogi) is one that sustains (or directs) the various functions of the created minds (through the incidental causes).

Explanation

The *Chitta* that arises out of repetition of *Mantra* has a different function than the *Chitta* that arises out of austerities. Similarly, the *Chitta* promoted by the incidental cause of medicinal herbs is different from the *Chitta* that arises out of meditation and *Samadhi*. These different transformations are sustained by the *Chitta* which is one and the same in its pure state. This one *Chitta* is the intrinsic state of all individual minds, and is attuned with *Mahat* or the Cosmic Mind.

Sutra 6

तत्र ध्यानजमनाशयम्

TATRA DHYANAJAM ANASHAYAM.

TATRA: Of these. DHYANAJAM: *Chitta* born of meditation (and *Samadhi*). ANASHAYAM: Free of Karmic impressions.

Meaning

Of these (five transformations as described in Sutra 1 of this chapter), the *Chitta* born of meditation (and *Samadhi*) is free of Karmic impressions.

Explanation

It has been explained how various incidental causes bring about transformations in the *Chitta*. But, of these, the transformation that is caused by meditation and *Samadhi* is the highest, since it destroys the seeds of Karmas, and thus, enables the Yogi to be liberated from the world-process.

The Karmas that are burnt up (destroyed) are explained in the following Sutra.

Sutra 7

कर्माशुक्लाकृष्णं योगिनस्त्रिविधमितरेषाम्

KARMA ASHUKLA AKRISHNAM YOGINAS TRIVIDHAM ITARESHAM.

KARMA: Action. ASHUKLA: Non-white (beyond virtue). AKRISHNAM: Non-black (beyond vice). YOGINAS: For Yogis. TRIVIDHAM: Of three kinds. ITARESHAM: Others.

Meaning

Karma is beyond virtue and vice for the Yogis, while it is of three types for others.

Explanation

A Yogi transcends all Karmas. He is beyond virtue and vice. But others are bound by Karmas that are of three types: virtuous, vicious and mixed. *Shukla Karmas* are actions that are in accordance with the rules of the *Yamas* and *Niyamas* — actions that give rise to virtuous impressions. *Krishna Karmas* are actions that are opposed to the *Yamas* and *Niyamas*; they are backed up by violence, falsehood and greed, and they give rise to sinful or unrighteous impressions. Those who are not Yogis are bound by *Shukla-Krishna Karmas* or mixed Karmas, a blend of virtuous Karmas that give rise to happiness and vicious Karmas that give rise to pain.

In the case of an enlightened Yogi, the *Kleshas* exist in him in *Dagdha Avastha* or the burnt up state, and therefore, his actions produce neither pleasure nor pain. A Sage performs actions without the sense of doership and enjoyership, and consequently, no new Karmas are generated. Established in the Self, he is beyond virtue and vice, and all his actions are called *Ashukla Akrishna* — neither white nor black.

CYCLE OF THE MIND

IMPRESSIONS
Samskaras

EXPERIENCE
Bhoga

SUBTLE DESIRES
Vasanas

ACTION
Karma

THOUGHT WAVES
Vrittis

DESIRES
Kama

Sutra 8

ततस्तद्विपाकानुगुणानामेवाभिव्यक्तिर्वासनानाम्

TATAS TAT VIPAKA ANUGUNANAM EVA ABHIVYAKTIR VASANANAM.

TATAH: Of these (three types of Karmas). TAT VIPAKA ANUGUNANAM: According to their fructification. EVA: Only. ABHIVYAKTIH: Manifest. VASANANAM: *Vasanas* or subtle desires.

Meaning

Only those subtle desires arise that correspond to the fructification of (the three types of) Karmas.

Explanation

Yogis who are established in the art of performing selfless actions (*Niskamya Karma*) perform Karmas for the purification of the *Chitta*. Those who are enlightened are established in the Self and are untouched by the fructifications of such Karmas. But the vast majority of people who perform actions with desire (*Sakamya Karma*) are confined to Karmic fructifications in the form of *Jati* (class), *Ayu* (life) and *Bhoga* (enjoyment). *(RAJA YOGA: II, 13)*

Vicious Karmas generate vicious *Samskaras* or impressions in the form of Karmic seeds. These *Samskaras* give rise to *Vasanas* or subtle desires, which are like sprouts. In turn, the *Vasanas* give rise to actions and experiences. From these Karmas (actions) new impressions are formed. Thus the cycle continues until a Yogi ends it by the attainment of *Viveka Khyati* or intuitional knowledge.

This Sutra explains that when a past good Karma is about to fructify, the subconscious becomes laden with auspicious subtle desires. Therefore, one enjoys an atmosphere of success, prosperity and favorable circumstances. On the other hand, if a negative Karma is about to fructify, the subconscious becomes tainted by inauspicious subtle desires and consequently, one is caught in an atmosphere of pain, misery, sorrow and degradation.

Sutra 9

जातिदेशकालव्यवहितानामप्यानन्तर्यं स्मृतिसंस्कारयोरेकरूपत्वात्

JATI DESH KALA VYAVAHITANAM API ANANTARYAM SMRITI SAMSKARAYOH EKARUPATWAT.

JATI: Class. DESH: Place. KALA: Time. VYAVAHITANAM: Being separated by. API: Yet. ANANTARYAM: Continuity. SMRITI: Memory. SAMSKARA: Impressions. EKARUPATWAT: Because of the unity of the two.

Meaning

Though separated by time, place and class, yet there is a continuity (in the subtle desires) because of the unity of memory and Karmic impressions.

Explanation

Karmas have been performed in different births, at different times, in different places, and yet, by the force of memory, those Karmas that are to fructify come together and give rise to corresponding *Vasanas* or subtle desires in the mind. This is due to the power of memory.

For example, human Karmas that are to fructify in a human embodiment blend together even though the embodiments in which they were generated might not have been consecutive. A person might have been a human being three embodiments before, and yet, the Karmas generated during the immediate three animal embodiments are held back, while the Karmas of the past human embodiment are awakened by the force of memory. In the same way, in an animal embodiment, the Karmas of any human embodiment are held back while the memory operating through the present animal body draws Karmic impressions of similar animal embodiments of the past.

Even in daily life, when a person meets a childhood friend after the lapse of 20 or more years, he remembers many experiences of old times, while the memories based upon recent experiences are held back. Such is the law of association based on memory. Therefore, *Samskaras* and the function of memory go together giving rise to the continuity of the subtle desires which coexist with the fructifying Karmas.

Sutra 10

तासामनादित्वं चाशिषो नित्यत्वात्

TASAM ANADITWAM CHA ASHISHAH NITYATWAT.

TASAM: Of those subtle desires. ANADITWAM: There is beginninglessness. CHA: And. ASHISHAH: The desire to exist. NITYATWAT: Being eternal.

Meaning

The desire to exist being eternal, these subtle desires are beginningless.

233

Explanation

When did the soul enter into Karmic entanglement? When did the *Vasanas* or subtle desires begin? When was the first embodiment of the soul and why? Such questions cannot be answered in terms of the conditioned human mind.

The fact is, ignorance is beginningless; the soul also is beginningless, which is inferred from the fact that everyone wishes to exist forever; no one can ever imagine his nonexistence. Therefore, the spirit has passed through countless embodiments from beginningless time.

This proves that the *Vasanas* are beginningless and have been formed through countless embodiments. However, ignorance, though being beginningless, comes to an end by knowledge, and consequently, the *Vasanas* are also destroyed. This leads to the Liberation of the soul, and is further explained in the following Sutra.

Sutra 11

हेतुफलाश्रयालम्बनै: संग्रहीतत्वादेषामभावे तदभाव:

HETU PHALA ASHRAYA ALAMBANAIH SANGRIHITATWAT ESHAM ABHAVE TADABHAVAH.

HETU: Cause. PHALA: Fructification or fruit. ASHRAYA: Receptacle. ALAMBANAIH: Support (by these). SANGRIHITATWAT: The subtle desires are formed, therefore. ESHAM: Of these (four). ABHAVE: Being absent. TADABHAVAH: The subtle desires become absent (cease to exist).

Meaning

These four give rise to the formation of subtle desires: cause, fructification, receptacle, and support; therefore, when these are destroyed, the *Vasanas* become extinct.

Explanation

This Sutra sums up various points referring to the *Vasanas* (subtle desires), which have been explained before. To reiterate, an aspirant must gain a deep insight into the following four factors that go to constitute the existence of the *Vasanas*.

1. *Hetu* or cause of *Vasanas*. Ignorance and its immediate effects, consisting of the five *Kleshas* or afflictions, are the cause of *Sakamya Karmas* or actions performed with desire. These, in turn, give rise to the formation of subtle desires. *Kleshas*, *Vasanas* and Karmas go to form a vicious circle. *(RAJA YOGA: II, 3-9)*

2. *Phala* or fruit (Karmic fructifications). *Sakamya Karmas* give rise to three types of fruit: *Jati* (class), *Ayu* (life) and *Bhoga* (experiences of pleasure and pain). *(RAJA YOGA: II, 13)*

3. *Ashraya* or receptacle. The unenlightened *Chitta* that has not yet accomplished its purpose by giving rise to *Viveka Khyati* or intuitional knowledge, is referred to as the receptacle of *Vasanas*.

4. *Alambana* or support. The objects of the senses are the support or sustenance for the *Vasanas*.

The beginningless *Vasanas* are coexistent with these four. As long as they are present, the *Vasanas* continue to be formed in the unconscious. But when they are destroyed by the force of *Viveka Khyati* or intuitive knowledge, the *Vasanas*, like a river that is no longer fed by its source or its tributaries, becomes extinct. *(RAJA YOGA: IV: 30)*

The disciplines of Yoga are directed towards the removal of ignorance by the unfoldment of *Viveka Khyati*. When ignorance is destroyed, the accompanying *Kleshas* are also destroyed. They attain the state of *Dagdha Bija* (burnt up seed). In the case of an enlightened Sage, his *Chitta* has already accomplished the purpose of its existence, and therefore, it begins to melt in its source. *(RAJA YOGA: IV, 34)*

Endowed with an enlightened *Chitta*, such a liberated Sage is no longer influenced by impressions arising out of sense-perceptions. Therefore, the senses that constantly feed the river of *Vasanas* in the ignorant are as if absent in a Sage.

The process of destruction of *Vasanas* is progressive. Impure *Vasanas* are destroyed by pure *Vasanas*, and in turn, even these pure *Vasanas* become extinct, like a fire that has become extinct with the exhaustion of its fuel. Thus a Yogi becomes absolutely free from the bondage of beginningless desires.

Sutra 12

अतीतानागतं स्वरूपतोऽस्त्यध्वभेदाद्धर्माणाम्

ATITA ANAGATAM SWARUPATAH ASTI ADHWABHEDAT DHARMANAM.

ATITA: Past. ANAGATAM: Future. SWARUPATAH ASTI: Remain in the form of. ADHWABHEDAT: Because differences are caused by time. DHARMANAM: Of the *Dharmas*.

Meaning

Since the differences in *Dharmas* are caused by time, they exist in the form of past and future.

Explanation

According to the theory of causation sustained by *Raja Yoga*, a cause does not give birth to a new effect, for in that case, the new effect would have proceeded from nothing, which is contrary to reason. For example, a pot that is an effect of a clod of earth is ever latent in the clod of earth; by the instrumentality of a potter, the pot comes to exist (nothing new is born), and with the passage of time the manifestation of pot passes on to an unmanifest state without affecting the basic cause — the clod of earth.

In the same manner, *Vasanas* arise out of the *Chitta* and dissolve in the *Chitta*. Any differences are caused by time. The *Vasanas* that are operative at the present will pass on to the realms of the past, while the *Vasanas* that have not yet come will arise in the future.

The Sutra implies that as long as the *Chitta* (*Dharmi*) exists, the *Vasanas* will continue to exist in one form of another. But with the dissolution of the *Chitta* into *Prakriti*, there is no more manifestation of *Vasanas*, and as a result, the Spirit or *Purusha* becomes free from the world-process.

Sutra 13

ते व्यक्तसूक्ष्मा गुणात्मानः

TE VYAKTA SUKSHMA GUNATMANAH.

TE: These (*Dharmas*). VYAKTA: Manifest. SUKSHMA: Subtle or unmanifest. GUNATMANAH: Of the nature of the *Gunas*.

Meaning

All these (*Dharmas*), whether manifest or unmanifest, are of the nature of the *Gunas*.

Explanation

Prakriti or Nature is the supreme *Dharmi* which brings forth the various effects or *Dharmas*. All evolutes of *Prakriti*, from *Mahat* (Cosmic Mind) to the five gross elements, are *Dharmas*, which either exists in a manifest form or in an unmanifest form. *(RAJA YOGA: III, 14)*

In other words, with deeper analysis, the five gross elements are nothing but the five subtle elements, and these, as well as the eleven *Indriyas*, are in turn nothing but the *Ahamkara Tattwa* (ego-principle). *Ahamkara Tattwa* in its deeper analysis, is the same as *Mahat Tattwa* (Cosmic Mind), and the latter is nothing but *Prakriti* consisting of the three *Gunas*. Thus, the entire world-process is composed of the *Gunas*, the *Dharmi* or the basic stuff, of which, from a broad point of view, all effects are *Dharmas*. Therefore, Liberation consists of being free from the three *Gunas* and their effects.

Sutra 14

परिणामैकत्वाद्वस्तुतत्त्वम्

PARINAMA EKATWAT VASTU TATWAM.

PARINAMA: Modification. EKATWAT: Being unified. VASTU TATWAM: Objects appear as such.

Meaning

Because of the unity of modifications, the (distinct) objects appear as such.

Explanation

A question can be asked that since the three *Gunas* are mutually conflicting in their natures, how is it that they give rise to specific modifications? Further, since all objects are made up of only the three *Gunas*, why should there be any differentiation among them?

The answer is that since the three *Gunas* become unified in their modifications, they cause the modification of a particular object, and since they are unified in different proportions, they give rise to numerous objects. For example, earth, water and sun, in spite of being different from each other, through the unity of modifications, give rise to a specific tree.

Sutra 15

वस्तुस.म्ये चित्तभेदात्तयोर्विभक्त: पन्था:

VASTU SAMYE CHITTA BHEDAT TAYOR VIBHAKTAH PANTHAH.

VASTU: Object. SAMYE: Unity. CHITTA: Mind-stuff. BHEDAT: Because of differences. TAYOH: Of both (*Chitta* and the objects perceived by it). VIBHAKTAH: Different or separate from each other. PANTHAH: Ways.

Meaning

In spite of the unity of the object, (it is perceived differently) because of differences among the *Chittas* (conditioned minds), the object and the (perceiving) *Chitta* both have separate ways.

Explanation

Though an object is one, yet different *Chittas* hold different attitudes towards it. For example, gold is loved by the greedy, renounced by ascetics, and is seen as insignificant by the wise. A young lady is embraced with affection by her father, viewed lustfully by her lover, and is seen with a dispassionate attitude by a renunciate. Therefore, although both the *Chitta* and the objects coexist with each other, yet they are different from each other.

Both the *Chitta* and the objects of the world have evolved out of *Mahat* (Cosmic Mind), which in turn has evolved out of *Prakriti* consisting of the three *Gunas*. In spite of the fact that they (the *Chitta* and the objects) are constituted of the three *Gunas* in their final analysis, yet they are different from each other. *Chitta* in its purified state communes with *Mahat*. In its unenlightened state, there are many *Chittas* (conditioned minds), and each one has become a limiting medium for each individual soul (*Purusha*).

Purusha in essence is ever free, infinite and eternal, but because of its identification with the *Chitta*, it has become individualized and has entered into a world-process of repeated birth and death. These points are explained in the following Sutras.

Sutra 16

न चैकचित्ततन्त्रं वस्तु तदप्रमाणकं तदा किं स्यात्

NA CHA EKA CHITTA TANTRAM VASTU TAT APRAMANAKAM TADA KIM SYAT.

NA: Not. CHA: In addition to this. EKA CHITTA TANTRAM: Under the control of one *Chitta*. VASTU: Object. TAT: That. APRAMANAKAM: Without the valid cognition of *Chitta*. TADA: Then. KIM SYAT: What will happen to the object.

Meaning

In addition to this, the objects are not under the control of one *Chitta*, because, when a *Chitta* of a person does not cognize an object (turns away from it), what will happen to the object?

Explanation

If objects depend upon one *Chitta*, then when that *Chitta* becomes enlightened, its objects must vanish; and even if that *Chitta* turns its attention away from one object and directs it towards another,

241

the former object will vanish. But this is not the case in practical reality — while one mind withdraws its attention from one object, there are many other minds that continue to cognize the object. Therefore, objects exist independent of the perceiving mind in an individual. This Sutra refutes the view of Subjective Idealism as maintained by *Vijnana Vadins* (a Buddhistic school of philosophy).

Sutra 17

तदुपरागापेक्षित्वाच्चित्तस्य वस्तु ज्ञाताज्ञातम्

TAT UPARAGA APEKSHITATWAT CHITTASYA JNATA AJNATAM.

TAT: That. **UPARAGA**: Influence (coloring). **APEKSHITATWAT**: Dependent upon. **CHITTASYA**: Of the mind. **JNATA**: Known. **AJNATAM**: Unknown.

Meaning

The *Chitta* depends upon being influenced (by the object), therefore, the object is either known or unknown.

Explanation

When the senses come into contact with an object, they bring perceptions of the object to the *Chitta*, which then becomes modified into the form of the object (*Vishayakara Vritti*). The *Purusha* or the Self reflecting in the *Chitta* then causes the cognition of the object — "I know the object." On the other hand, when the senses are not in contact with an object, the *Chitta* cannot assume the form of the object, and therefore, the object is unknown.

So far it has been shown that the *Chitta* is different from the objects. The next Sutra shows that the *Purusha* is distinct from the *Chitta* — the *Purusha* being eternal while the *Chitta* is everchanging.

Sutra 18

सदा ज्ञाताश्चित्तवृत्तयस्तःप्रभोः पुरुषस्यापरिणामित्वात्

SADA JNATAH CHITTA VRITTAYAH TAT PRABHOH PURUSHASYA APARINAMITWAT.

SADA: Always. JNATAH: Known. CHITTA VRITTAYAH: The *Vrittis* of the *Chitta*. TAT PRABHOH: Is master or lord. PURUSHASYA: Of the Self. APARINAMITWAT: Because of being unchanging in nature.

Meaning

The *Vrittis* of the *Chitta* are ever known to its Lord, the Self, because the latter is ever unchanging.

Explanation

The changes in the *Vrittis* or thought-waves of the mind are perceived by the unchanging Spirit or Self. If the Self were also a changing principle, then changes of the mind could not be perceived, for changes are valid only with relation to an unchanging center.

Purusha is the witness of the *Vrittis* of the *Chitta*. It is the duty of the *Chitta* to become modified into the object, and to present its modified form before its lord and master, the *Purusha*. And even in the absence of objects, the *Chitta* presents itself in its own form before the *Purusha*. Therefore, since the *Purusha* is ever aware of the *Chitta* and its modifications by reflecting itself in the *Chitta*, the knowledge of the *Chitta* and its functions do not cause any change in the *Purusha*.

The drift of the Sutra is that the *Purusha* is ever distinct from the *Chitta*. This is further explained in the following Sutra.

Sutra 19

न तत्स्वाभासं दृश्यत्वात्

NA TAT SWABHASAM DRISHYATWAT.

NA: Not. TAT: That (*Chitta*). SWABHASAM: Self-luminous. DRISHYATWAT: Being of the nature of the "seen."

Meaning

The *Chitta* is not self-luminous, being of the nature of the "seen."

Explanation

All the evolutes of *Prakriti* come in the range of the "seen," while *Purusha* is the only "seer." The senses perceive objects by the light borrowed from the *Chitta*, and in turn, the *Chitta* borrows light from the *Purusha*. The *Purusha* does not need to borrow light from any other source; It is self-luminous.

The *Purusha* identified with the *Chitta* says, "I am unhappy or I am happy, I am angry or I am peaceful." Pleasure, pain, anger and serenity are all modifications of the *Chitta*, which are in turn "seen" by the *Purusha*.

If it is said that *Chitta* brings about the knowledge of objects as well as the knowledge of itself (i.e., happiness, pain, sorrow, etc.) without the *Purusha*, it is not so. The following Sutra explains.

Sutra 20

एकसमये चोभयानवधारणम्

EKA SAMAYE CHOBHAYA ANAVADHARANAM.

EKA SAMAYE: At one time. CHA: And. UBHAYA: Both. ANAVADHARANAM: Cannot be known.

Meaning

Both (the *Chitta* and the objects) cannot be known (by the *Chitta*) at one time.

Explanation

If there were no assistance from the *Purusha*, the *Chitta* could not accomplish the perceptions of itself and its objects at the same time. But in practical life it is seen that a person is aware of his mental condition (his *Chitta*) through experiences of pleasure, pain and the like, while at the same time he is also aware of the objects of the world. Since such is the case, it proves that *Purusha*, which is distinct from the *Chitta*, accomplishes the task of all perceptions.

Sutra 21

चित्तान्तरदृश्ये बुद्धिबुद्धेरतिप्रसङ्गः स्मृतिसंकरश्च

CHITTANTAR DRISHYE BUDDHIH BUDDHEH ATIPRASANGAH SMRITI SANKARASHCHA.

CHITTANTAR DRISHYE: By presuming that one *Chitta* is "seen" by another *Chitta*. BUDDHIH BUDDHEH: *Chitta* of the *Chitta*. ATIPRASANGAH: Unending series. SMRITI SANKARASHCHA: And also there will be confusion in memory.

Meaning

By presuming that one *Chitta* is "seen" by another *Chitta*, then there will not only be an unending series of *Chittas* of the *Chitta*, but also confusion in memory.

Explanation

If one *Chitta* is considered as the perceiver of another *Chitta*, then this will lead to an unending series, for the perceiving *Chitta* will in turn need another *Chitta* to perceive it, and so on *ad infinitum*. Further, since each *Chitta* in this endless series will become the basis of one's impressions, there will be a great confusion in the function of memory. Therefore, it is evident that the *Chitta* is perceived by the *Purusha*, who is self-luminous and distinct from the *Chitta*.

Sutra 22

चितेरप्रतिसंक्रमायास्तदाकारापत्तौ स्वबुद्धिसंवेदनम्

CHITEH APRATISANKRAMAYAS TAT AKARA APATTAU SWABUDDHI SAMVEDANAM.

CHITEH: The *Purusha* (the conscious being). APRATISANKRAMAYAH: Who is free of actions and modifications. TAT AKARA APATTAU: Being identified with that (the *Chitta*). SWABUDDHI: Its own *Chitta*. SAMVEDANAM: Perceives.

Meaning

Though the *Purusha* (the conscious being) is free of actions and modifications, yet because of being identified with that (*Chitta*), It is able to know its own *Chitta*.

Explanation

A doubt may arise that if the *Purusha* is unchanging and eternal, then how can It know the *Chitta*? Because, by knowing the *Chitta*, the *Purusha* must allow itself to be involved in the function of knowing, and this would render the *Purusha* subject to changes.

This Sutra explains that the *Purusha* knows the *Chitta* by becoming identified with it. It is similar to the sun being reflected in a mirror and illumining objects inside a room; though the objects are illumined by the reflected sun within the mirror, the reality behind the reflection is the sun that abides in the sky.

The reflection of the *Purusha* in the *Chitta* causes the perception of the *Chitta* and its functions; but the *Purusha* in itself is ever unchanging and eternal. In other words, the *Chitta* that has reflected the *Purusha* brings about the duality of seer and seen; in reality the *Purusha* is not the seer or knower or experiencer, rather it is Pure Consciousness itself.

Sutra 23

द्रष्टृदृश्योपरक्तं चित्तं सर्वार्थम्

DRASTRI DRISHYA UPARAKTAM CHITTAM SARVARTHAM.

DRASTRI: The Seer. DRISHYA: The seen. UPARAKTAM: Colored. CHITTAM: The mind-stuff. SARVARTHAM: Assumes all forms (seems to cognize all).

Meaning

Colored by the Seer and the seen, the *Chitta* assumes all forms.

Explanation

The *Chitta* is, in fact, different from both the objects and the *Purusha*. But due to the fact that *Sattwa* is more predominate in the *Chitta*, the latter is like transparent crystal which seems to be identified with anything placed near it. On one side the *Chitta* is able to reflect the *Purusha*, giving rise to the illusion that the *Chitta* in itself is the *Purusha*, while on the other side it reflects the objects of the world and becomes colored by them, giving rise to the illusion that the *Chitta* is inseparably related to the objects.

The following Sutra gives additional reason to support the view that the *Purusha* is different from the *Chitta*.

Sutra 24

तदसंख्येयवासनाभिश्चित्रमपि परार्थं संहत्यकारित्वात्

TAT ASAMKHYEYA VASANABHIH CHITRAMAPI PARARTHAM SAMHATYAKARITWAT.

TAT: It (the *Chitta*). ASAMKHYEYA: Numerous. VASANABHIH: By subtle desires. CHITRAMAPI: Being colored. PARARTHAM: Meant for another (for *Purusha*). SAMHATYAKARITWAT: Because it acts in a coordinated form.

Meaning

Because it (the *Chitta*) acts in a coordinated form, though it is colored by countless subtle desires, yet it is meant for another (the *Purusha*).

Explanation

It is seen in general parlance that any object which performs its function in conjunction with many other objects is serving something other than itself. For example, many objects blend together when food is prepared, and the food is meant for an enjoyer different from itself. Many objects such as bricks, cement, and the like, have been worked together in constructing a house; and the house is meant to be enjoyed by someone else.

In the same way, although the *Chitta* functions in conjunction with the objects and the senses, it exists to serve the *Purusha*; it does not exist for itself. Therefore, the distinction between the *Chitta* and the *Purusha* has been shown by adopting intellectual reasoning. But the direct realization of this fact is possible only when a Yogi enters into *Samadhi* and discovers it by his intuitional vision. This is shown in the following Sutra.

Sutra 25

विशेषदर्शिन आत्मभावभावनाविनिवृत्ति:

VISHESHA DARSHINAH ATMABHAVA BHAVANA VINIVRITTIH.

VISHESHA DARSHINAH: He who is endowed with intuitive vision arising out of *Samadhi*. ATMABHAVA BHAVANA: Various attitudes concerning the Self. VINIVRITTIH: Removal.

Meaning

For the Yogi who is endowed with intuitional vision, the various attitudes pertaining to the Self are completely removed.

Explanation

Guided by scriptures, an aspirant tries to think of the Self in various ways. He meditates upon Its various attributes such as eternity, infinity, immortality, all-knowingness, omnipotence and others. He enquires into the nature of the Self by, "Who am I? Whence am I? Etc." These concepts and attitudes are known as *Atmabhava Bhavana*.

As long as intuitional knowledge (*Viveka Khyati*) has not been attained, the mind of a Yogi continues to maintain these various concepts about the Self. But when intuitional knowledge is unfolded during *Samadhi* resulting in actual realization of the Self, all these concepts are removed and transcended.

Sutra 26

तदाविवेकनिम्नं कैवल्यप्राग्भारं चित्तम्

TADA VIVEKANIMNAM KAIVALYA PRAGBHARAM CHITTAM.

TADA: Then. VIVEKANIMNAM: Bent low with discriminative knowledge. KAIVALYA PRAGBHARAM: Flowing towards *Kaivalya*. CHITTAM: The mind-stuff.

Meaning

Then, the *Chitta* of a Yogi, bent low with (the burden of) discriminative knowledge, flows towards *Kaivalya* (Liberation).

Explanation

During the state of ignorance, the mind-stuff in a person is burdened with worldly impressions, thereby making it flow only towards the increasing entanglements of the world. But when a Yogi ascends the heights of *Samadhi*, his mind bends low with discriminative knowledge and flows towards Liberation. Just as a river that has descended from a mountainous height flows impetuously to the ocean, in the same way, when the *Chitta* has ascended the mountainous heights of *Samadhi*, it turns into a stream of knowledge, and, descending with increasing momentum, flows into the ocean of Liberation.

Sutra 27

तच्छिद्रेषु प्रत्ययान्तराणि संस्कारेभ्यः

TAT CHHIDRESHU PRATYAYANTARANI SAMSKAREBHYAH.

TAT: That (*Samadhi*). CHHIDRESHU: In the intervals. PRATYAYANTARANI: The knowledge of other objects. SAMSKAREBHYAH: By the previous *Samskaras* or impressions.

Meaning

During the intervals of *Samadhi* (the *Asamprajnata*) the knowledge of other objects arises due to previous (outgoing) impressions.

Explanation

In an enlightened Yogi, while his *Chitta* flows towards Liberation, there are apparent interruptions in the flow caused by the presence of *Vyutthana Samskaras* (impressions of outgoing mind). These impressions enable a Yogi to sustain the practical realities of life, but since they exist in the *Dagdha Bija* or burnt up state, they do not cause new Karmas or entanglements. This Sutra applies to the state of *Jivanmukti* (Liberation in life).

Sutra 28

हानमेषां क्लेशवदुक्तम्

HANAM ESHAM KLESHAVAT UKTAM.

HANAM: Destruction. ESHAM: Of these. KLESHAVAT: Similar to the afflictions. UKTAM: Has been already said.

Meaning

These impressions are also destroyed, as in the case of the *Kleshas*, which has already been explained before.

Explanation

It has been stated in Sutra 10 of *Sadhana Pad* that the *Kleshas* are reduced to the state of burnt up seeds by the practice of *Kriya Yoga* and other Yogic disciplines, and then the *Chitta* itself is allowed to be dissolved in its cause (*Prakriti*). The same fact is explained in this Sutra in reference to outgoing impressions.

These subtle impressions of the *Vyutthana* states of mind which exist in a liberated Sage are also destroyed when the very *Chitta* of the Sage follows the process of involution and becomes merged in *Prakriti*. This Sutra applies to the state of *Videhamukti* or disembodied Liberation. (RAJA YOGA: I, 51)

Sutra 29

प्रसंख्यानेऽप्यकुसीदस्य सर्वथा विवेकख्यातेर्धर्ममेघः समाधिः

PRASANKHYANE API AKUSIDASYA SARVATHA VIVEKA KHYATER DHARMA MEGHAH SAMADHIH.

PRASANKHYANE: Towards intuitional knowledge. API: Even. AKUSIDASYA: He who has developed dispassion. SARVATHA: At all times or ceaselessly. VIVEKA KHYATEH: By the discriminative knowledge. DHARMA MEGHAH: Cloud of virtue. SAMADHIH: Superconsciousness.

Meaning

The Yogi who is dispassionate even towards intuitional knowledge (*Viveka Khyati* that arises during *Sasmita Samadhi*), through the ceaseless flow of the same, attains *Dharma Megha Samadhi*.

Explanation

It has been explained in *Samadhi Pad* that when a Yogi advances in the path of *Sasmita Samadhi*, which is the highest limit of lower (*Samprajnata*) *Samadhi*, he experiences *Viveka Khyati* or intuitional knowledge due to the increasing purity of the *Chitta*. If this intuitional knowledge is maintained ceaselessly and without any obstruction, a Yogi develops *Para Vairagya* or supreme dispassion. He begins to see his Spirit as distinct from his *Chitta*, and therefore, he develops a mystic inclination to turn away from the *Chitta* itself.

This state has two aspects: Firstly, the flow of intuitional knowledge becomes increasingly firm and unobstructed, and secondly, the impressions of *Nirodha Samadhi* (or *Asamprajnata Samadhi*, the highest form of superconsciousness) are developed. These impressions destroy all other impressions, and they are figuratively described as *Dharma Megha* or the "Cloud of Virtue," which rains down the nectar of immortality (Liberation). These nectarine showers of virtue bring about the end of the burning fever of the afflictions in the heart of a Yogi, thus leading him to *Kaivalya*.

It should be noted that the virtue of *Dharma Megha* is not virtue in a relative sense; rather, the highest form of virtue is in terms of *Nirodha*

Samskaras or impressions of control. Further, *Dharma Megha Samadhi*, *Para Vairagya*, and *Nirodha Samadhi* actually occur simultaneously; they are described to occur in sequence only to aid the aspirant to view the same state from different perspectives. *(RAJA YOGA: I, 16)*

The result of *Dharma Megha Samadhi* is further described in the following Sutra.

Sutra 30

ततः क्लेशकर्मनिवृत्तिः

TATAH KLESHA KARMA NIVRITTIH.

TATAH: By that (Cloud of Virtue). KLESHA: Afflictions. KARMA: Actions. NIVRITTIH: Are removed or destroyed.

Meaning

By that (Cloud of Virtue), the afflictions and Karmic entanglements are destroyed (in their totality).

Explanation

The five *Kleshas* and their effects, the three types of Karma (white, black and mixed), are destroyed as a result of the experience of *Dharma Megha*. A Yogi becomes established in the Self by the constant practice of *Asamprajnata Samadhi* and is no longer bound by the wheel of birth and death.

Sutra 31

तदा सर्वांवरणमलापेतस्य ज्ञानस्यानन्त्याज्ज्ञेयमल्पम्

TADA SARVA AVARANAM ALAPETASYA JNANASYA ANANTYAT JNEYAM ALPAM.

TADA: Then. SARVA: All forms of. AVARANAM: Veils. ALAPETASYA: Of which (all veils) have been removed. JNANASYA: Of knowledge. ANANTYAT: Being endless or limitless. JNEYAM: The knowable. ALPAM: Becomes little.

Meaning

Then (as a result of *Dharma Megha Samadhi*) when all the veils of illusion are lifted, the knowledge (in a Yogi) becomes limitless, while the knowable is rendered little or insignificant.

Explanation

As long as a Yogi has not experienced intuitional knowledge (*Viveka Khyati*), his knowledge is conditioned by *Avidya* or ignorance. During this state of ignorance, the knowable, i.e., the objects of the world, is limitless before his vision. And in his vain effort to know these objects, he continues to tumble through numerous embodiments.

Yoga Vasistha tells a parable about three princes, the sons of a great king, who decided to measure the extent of the universe. They practised intense austerity with the desire of gaining the possibility to travel at immense speeds in order to be able to reach the utmost limits of the universe. As a result of their austerity, they were granted a speed that was greater than anything conceivable in this world. Then, with their immense speed, they began to roam through creation. The storyteller says that even though thousands of years have rolled on, those princes are still sojourning through the universe, and they have not yet covered even a small portion of creation.

But even though in the realm of ignorance the world of knowable objects is limitless, yet as a Yogi ascends the heights of wisdom through *Samadhi*, the world begins to shrink before his vision. And when his intuition blooms into perfection, the world of knowable objects becomes insignificant. In other words, the relative world-process is transcended, and he has nothing more to know.

The knowledge wherein the triad of seer, seen and sight has dissolved is the giver of Liberation. It shines like the midday sun in a cloudless sky, before the effulgence of which all intellectual forms of knowledge, like the stars of the sky, pale into insignificance.

How is it then that the everchanging *Gunas* do not overpower the enlightened Yogi, again bringing about a state of bondage for him? This is explained in the following Sutra.

Sutra 32

ततः कृतार्थानां परिणामक्रमसमाप्तिर्गुणानाम्

TATAH KRITARTHANAM PARINAMKRAMA SAMAPTIH GUNANAM.

TATAH: Then. KRITARTHANAM: Those who are fulfilled (through Liberation). PARINAMKRAMA: The series of changes or modifications. SAMAPTIH: Come to an end. GUNANAM: Of the three *Gunas*.

Meaning

Then (after the experience of *Dharma Megha Samadhi*) for the Yogis who have accomplished the purpose of their existence (through Liberation), the series of modifications of the *Gunas* cease to exist.

Explanation

It has been explained before that *Prakriti* consisting of the three *Gunas* exists for the purpose of giving the soul *Bhoga* (enjoyment) and *Apavarga* (Liberation). Although these *Gunas* and their modifications continue to operate for souls that are unenlightened, keeping them in a state of bondage, yet once Enlightenment is attained, a Yogi becomes free of them and their series of modifications, thereby freeing him from the series of births and deaths.

Prakriti is ever changing, but in the case of the Enlightened these changes are from similar to similar, like the burning flame of a candle. In the case of the unenlightened, however, the changes are complex and dissimilar. The latter type of changes are the basis for the soul's dependence in the world of matter, while the former are ineffective in causing bondage for the soul.

The term *Krama*, meaning "series," is now explained.

Sutra 33

क्षणप्रतियोगी परिणामापरान्तनिर्ग्राह्यः क्रमः

KSHANA PRATIYOGI PARINAMA APARANTA NIRGRAHYAH KRAMAH.

KSHANA PRATIYOGI: That which is related to the flow of moments. PARINAMA: Modification. APARANTA: End. NIRGRAHYAH: Perceptible. KRAMAH: Series.

Meaning

"Series" (*Krama*) is the flow of moments which are dependent upon the perception of the end of each modification.

Explanation

Changes continue in all objects ceaselessly, bringing about a series of modifications. These modifications are perceived by the person in the terms of a series of moments. Every modification is a result of many changes, and therefore is an end of a process. A series or *Krama* refers to a succession of modifications which are perceived in terms of a succession of moments.

Perception of *Krama* and the *Vrittis* of the *Chitta* are coexistent. In the state of *Kaivalya* (Liberation) the very *Chitta* itself is transcended, therefore, *Krama* terminates for a Yogi; consequently, a Yogi goes beyond all changes that occur through time and space.

Sutra 34

पुरुषार्थशून्यानां गुणानां प्रतिप्रसवः कैवल्यं स्वरूपप्रतिष्ठा वा चितिशक्तेरिति

PURUSHARTHA SHUNYANAM GUNANAM
PRATIPRASAVAH KAIVALYAM SWARUPA
PRATISTHA VA CHITISHAKTER ITI.

PURUSHARTHA: Purpose of the soul (goal of
self-effort). SHUNYANAM: Void. GUNANAM: Of
the *Gunas* of *Prakriti*. PRATIPRASAVAH:
Involution in their source. KAIVALYAM:
Independence or Liberation. SWARUPA
PRATISTHA: Establishment in the Self. VA: Or.
CHITISHAKTEH: Of the Seer (the power of
consciousness). ITI: Thus ends (the Sutras of *Raja
Yoga*).

Meaning

Devoid of serving any purpose for the soul, the
Gunas become involved in their own source (*Prakriti*),
or (in other words) the Seer (characterized by the
power of consciousness) becomes established in its
essential nature (the Self); thus ends the scripture of
Yoga.

Explanation

The *Gunas* of *Prakriti* continue to operate for
the sake of the *Purusha*. They must continue to
provide *Bhoga* (experiences of pleasure and pain) in
order to lead the soul to the ascending heights of
wisdom, until it attains *Apavarga* (Liberation). Once
in the state of Liberation, this twofold purpose
becomes extinct; the Yogi has attained the supreme
purpose of his existence, and there is nothing more to
be accomplished. *(RAJA YOGA: II, 27)*

Once the *Gunas* have returned to their source (*Prakriti*), the Spirit or *Purusha*, which has been identified with the *Vrittis* of the *Chitta*, is no longer under the influence of *Avidya* or ignorance. Therefore, it abides in its essential nature. This is known as Liberation.

This glorious state of human existence is the goal of all religious and mystical movements of this world. Though it is one and the same, yet it is known by different names according to the different religious and philosophical systems. Self-realization, Liberation, *Mukti*, *Nirvana*, Absolute Freedom, Independence, the Kingdom of Heaven, Communion with God, etc., are all synonymous, and convey the same meaning.

There is an important quotation from the *Vedas*, "*Ekam Sat Vipra Bahudha Vadanti*" — "The Truth is one, but the Sages speak of it in various ways." Therefore, there is no basic contradiction in different approaches to the same goal. Though apparently different in their approach, both the philosophical systems of Yoga and Vedanta are the same when deeply studied. Their apparent differences are meant to suit different types of aspirants; further, they do not contradict the disciplinary process of Yoga, rather, the practical insights presented in Yoga, and the philosophical insights of Vedanta are mutually supplementary and complementary to each other.

Prakriti of *Raja Yoga* is transmuted into the concept of *Maya* in Vedanta Philosophy; and since *Maya* is nothing but cosmic illusion, a Liberated Yogi is no longer deluded by it. Further, while *Raja Yoga* views all modifications of *Prakriti* in a realistic sense,

Vedanta explains them in the form of illusory superimpositions, like a snake seen in a rope during darkness. The effects of *Maya* (the mind, intellect, elements, and all manifested creation) are of the nature of *Maya* — illusory in nature; therefore, behind all names and forms, there is only one reality — the Self. That Self alone exists. A Sage who has attained this enlightenment becomes free of the bondage of the world-process; freed of all misery, established in its essential spiritual identity, the Spirit becomes immersed in the ocean of bliss.

Thus ends the fourth chapter
known as Kaivalya Pad
in the Raja Yoga of Patanjali Maharshi.

Om Shantih Shantih Shantih.

FIVE STATES OF THE CHITTA

STATE	GUNA	SYMPTOM	CAUSES	INCLINATION	VRITTI	CLASS
1. Mudha (dull)	Tamas (inertia)	Sleep, delusion, fear, laziness	Lust, anger, greed, infatuation	Vice	Outgoing & all-sided	Lowest
2. Kshipta (distracted)	Rajas (activity)	Pain, worry, ficklemindedness, selfish actions	Attachment, hatred, selfishness	Virtue & vice	Outgoing & all-sided	General
3. Vikshipta (partially concentrated)	Mixed Sattwa (purity)	Joy, patience, virtuous qualities selfless actions	Selflessness, righteousness	Knowledge, virtue, dispassion, spiritual prosperity	Ingoing & beginning of Samadhi	Aspirants
4. Ekagrata (one-pointed)	Pure Sattwa	Increasing detachment	Lower dispassion	Wisdom	One-pointed & lower Samadhi	Yogis
5. Niruddha (controlled)	Involution of the Gunas	Abiding in the Self	Supreme dispassion	Kaivalya or Liberation	Controlled & higher Samadhi	Perfected Yogis

FOUR BASIC PRINCIPLES OF RAJA YOGA

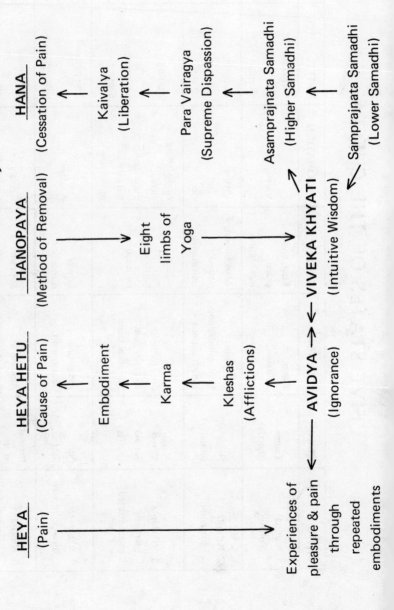

HEYA (Pain)	HEYA HETU (Cause of Pain)	HANOPAYA (Method of Removal)	HANA (Cessation of Pain)

Experiences of pleasure & pain through repeated embodiments → AVIDYA (Ignorance)

AVIDYA → VIVEKA KHYATI (Intuitive Wisdom)

Kleshas (Afflictions) → Karma → Embodiment →

Eight limbs of Yoga → VIVEKA KHYATI

VIVEKA KHYATI ← Asamprajnata Samadhi (Higher Samadhi) ← Samprajnata Samadhi (Lower Samadhi)

Kaivalya (Liberation) ← Para Vairagya (Supreme Dispassion) ← Asamprajnata Samadhi (Higher Samadhi) ← Samprajnata Samadhi (Lower Samadhi)

About the Author

Swami Jyotirmayananda was born on February 3, 1931, in Bihar, India. At the age of 22, he embraced the ancient order of Sanyasa as a disciple of the renowned Master Sri Swami Sivananda of the Divine Life Society in Rishikesh, India. Swamiji's great command of spiritual knowledge and dynamic expositions on Yoga and Vedanta philosophy attracted enormous interest and many requests for him to spread the spiritual knowledge of India in the West. In 1962, Swamij moved to Puerto Rico, and then in 1969 to Miami, where he established the Yoga Research Foundation.

Swami Jyotirmayananda is well recognized as one of the foremost proponents of Integral Yoga — a way of life and thought that synthesizes the various aspects of Yoga (Raja Yoga, Karma Yoga, Bhakti Yoga, and Jnana Yoga, in conjunction with Hatha Yoga) into a comprehensive plan of personality integration.

Also by Swami Jyotirmayananda

Vedic Scriptures with Commentary

Yoga Vasistha
Bhagavad Gita
Narada Bhakti Sutras

Yoga in Practice

Applied Yoga
Integral Yoga
Concentration & Meditation
The Art of Positive Thinking
The Art of Positive Feeling
The Four Gatekeepers at the Palace of Liberation
Advice to Students
Advice to Householders

Vedanta

Wisdom of the Upanishads
Jnana Yoga
Death & Reincarnation
Vedanta in Brief
Waking, Dream, & Deep Sleep

Mystical Insight

Mysticism of the Mahabharata
Mysticism of the Ramayana
Mysticism of the Srimad Bhagavatam
Mysticism of Devi Mahatmya
Mysticism of Hindu Gods & Goddesses

Hatha Yoga

Yoga Exercises for Health & Happiness
Beauty & Health through Yoga Relaxation

For a comprehensive list of books and digital media offered by the Yoga Research Foundation, please visit the online store at www.shop.yrf.org.